CONTEMPORARY ENGLISH
BOOK 1

Ardith Loustalet Simons

Kathleen Santopietro Weddel

CONTEMPORARY BOOKS

a division of NTC/CONTEMPORARY PUBLISHING GROUP
Lincolnwood, Illinois USA

Project Manager: Roseanne Mendoza
Cover Illustration: Regan Dunnick
Interior Illustrations: Amanda Duffy, Regan Dunnick, Jean Wisenbaugh

Acknowledgments

The authors and publisher would like to thank the following people for their help
and contribution to *Contemporary English:*
Series Consultant: **Catherine Porter,** Adult Learning Resource Center, Des Plaines, Illinois.
Reviewers: **Lisa Agao,** Resource Teacher, Fresno Adult School, Clovis, CA; **Bea Berrettini,**
Instructor, Fresno Adult School, Fresno, CA; **Lemuel S. Bonilla,** Professor, ESL, Santiago
Canyon College, Costa Mesa, CA; **Janice Bruno,** Instructor/Resource Teacher, Fresno Adult
School, Fresno, CA; **Mary Lou Byrne,** ESL Director, Triton College, River Grove, IL;
Clíf de Córdoba, Assistant Principal, Southgate Community Adult School, Los Angeles, CA;
Jill DeGrange, ESL Program Director, Salinas Adult School, Salinas, CA; **Samuela Eckstut,**
Senior Lecturer, CELOP, Boston University, Melrose, MA; **Stephen Ewert,** Instructor, Fresno
Adult School, Fresno, CA; **Eric Glicker,** Instructor, Rancho Santiago Community College District,
Santa Ana, CA; **Joyce Halenar,** Instructor/Advisor, Salinas Adult School, Salinas, CA; **Mary Jahr-
Purvis,** ESL Teacher, Salinas Adult School, Salinas, CA; **Robert Jenkins,** Assistant Professor,
Centennial Education Center, Santa Ana College, Santa Ana, CA; **Ruth Luman,** Instructor,
Long Beach Adult School, Long Beach, CA; **Sue Mendizza,** Coordinator, School of Continuing
Education, Santa Ana College, Santa Ana, CA; **Rachel Porcelli,** Independent Consultant, Dade
County, FL; **John Richardson,** Instructor, Fresno Adult School, Fresno, CA; **Judy Rosselli,**
VESL Instructor, San Diego Community College District, San Diego, CA; **Sandra Saldana,**
Lead Instructor, ESL Program, Triton College, River Grove, IL; **Kay Taggart,** Curriculum
Coordinator, Literacy and Workforce Development Center, El Paso Community College, El Paso,
TX; **Abigail H. Tom,** Instructor, Durham Technical Community College, Durham, NC.

Special thanks to **Jan Jarrell,** ESL Department Chair, Cesar Chavez Center, San Diego
Community College District, San Diego, CA, and **Donna Price Machado,** VESL Lab Coordinator,
San Diego Community College District, San Diego, CA.

ISBN: 0-8092-0703-6

Published by Contemporary Books,
a division of NTC/Contemporary Publishing Group, Inc.,
4255 West Touhy Avenue,
Lincolnwood (Chicago), Illinois 60712-1975 U.S.A.
© 1999 NTC/Contemporary Publishing Group, Inc.
All rights reserved. No part of this book may be reproduced,
stored in a retrieval system, or transmitted in any form or by any means,
electronic, mechanical, photocopying, recording, or otherwise,
without prior permission of the publisher.
Manufactured in the United States of America.

5 6 7 8 9 0 VLP VLP 0 5 4 3 2 1

CONTENTS

ABOUT THIS SERIES

PROGRAM COMPONENTS AND PHILOSOPHY

Contemporary English is a five-level interactive topic-based English-as-a-Second-Language series for adult learners ranging from the beginning-literacy level to the high-intermediate level. The series includes

- Student Books for classroom use

- Workbooks for independent use at home, in the classroom, or in a lab

- Audiocassettes for individual student, classroom, or lab use and

- Teacher's Manuals, with reproducible activity masters and unit progress checks for assessment.

These materials were correlated from inception to the California Model Standards for Adult ESL Programs, the MELT Student Performance Levels, and the SCANS (Secretary's Commission on Achieving Necessary Skills) Competencies.

Unique among adult ESL series, *Contemporary English* presents high-interest topics as a framework for developing a wide variety of language, thinking, and life skills. In addition to focusing on listening, speaking, reading, and writing skills, *Contemporary English* integrates work on language structures; problem-solving, critical-thinking, and graphic-literacy skills; and—increasingly important—work-related skills.

Contemporary English empowers students to take charge of their learning and to develop strong communication skills for the real world. For example, each unit in Books 1–4 falls under one of the following broad topics: Home and Neighborhood, People and Machines, Employment and Opportunity, Human Relations, Consumer Economics, Community Services, Transportation and Travel, Healthy Living, History and Geography, and Arts and Entertainment. (The lowest-level book, *Contemporary English* Literacy, addresses all of these topics except History and Geography and Arts and Entertainment.) In short, the series addresses topics of interest and concern to adult learners.

Contemporary English presents engaging and meaningful situations that provide a context for grammar structures, listening activities, and an emphasis on the world of work. Within this framework each unit offers a wealth of pair and group activities, often with designated team roles, and frequent individual and group presentations to the class. This approach mirrors the team organization characteristic of today's workplace and reflects the recent influence on education of the Department of Labor's SCANS report.

UNIT STRUCTURE OF THE STUDENT BOOKS

Contemporary English provides a controlled and predictable sequence of instruction and activities. Conveniently for teachers, each page of a unit functions as a self-contained mini-lesson. Each unit is divided into two parts, each of which begins with a **Scene** that presents, in comic-strip format, incidents from the lives of newcomers to the United States or aspects of U.S. culture that students encounter regularly. Lively, humorous, and dramatic, the **Scenes** engage students in the unit topics—usually by presenting typical problems in the lives of average people. A series of discussion questions proceeds from factual compre- hension of the **Scene** to personalization and, in Books 3 and 4, problem solving.

After each opening **Scene** comes **Sound Bites,** a focused listening task that includes pre-listening and post-listening work. **Sound Bites** presents target content and language structures through lively conver- sations and other samples of natural speech, such as telephone answering-machine messages and trans- portation announcements.

Throughout *Contemporary English*, grammar struc- tures are first contextualized in the **Scenes** and listening activities and then presented, practiced, and applied on follow-up **Spotlight** pages. Appearing two to four times in each unit, the **Spotlight** pages model target structures in contexts related to the unit topic. Special **Spotlight** feature boxes present the target structures schematically and provide brief, straightforward explanations when necessary. Exercises following the structure presentations allow students to manipulate the structures in meaningful contexts, such as stories or real-life situations. **Spotlight** pages usually end with a **Your Turn** and/or **In Your Experience** activity providing communicative application of the new structures.

These last two features, in addition to **Vocabulary Prompts,** occur within the units at the point of need, rather than in a fixed or unvarying part of each unit. **Vocabulary Prompts,** for example, serves to isolate challenging vocabulary before a listening or reading task. **Your Turn,** a follow-up to reading, listening, or structure practice, serves as a participatory task. **In Your Experience,** an activity drawing on students' prior knowledge and personal lives, allows learners to personalize the topics and relate them to their own experience.

Listening and speaking skills are developed further in the **Person to Person** activities, which present recorded two-person conversations exploring the unit topics in natural, colloquial language. Students listen to conversations, practice them, and work in pairs to complete a final open-ended dialogue. Students can then present their new conversations to the class.

Contemporary English helps students develop their reading skills and become motivated readers of English through **Reading for Real,** a page in each unit that provides stimulating authentic or adapted texts. With passages and realia that typically relate directly to the lives of characters in the **Scenes, Reading for Real** includes such real-life documents as a winning job résumé, instructions for office voice mail, biographies of real people, advice from the local police, and listings of music festivals around the country. Follow-up activities (such as **Your Turn** and **In Your Experience**) extend and personalize the reading.

Culture Corner provides further work on reading skills by focusing on the useful inside information about U.S. life that students love. Presented as brief readings typically paired with charts, graphics, or artwork, **Culture Corner** gives students the information they need to adapt to a culture that can often be confusing and difficult to understand. Interactive follow-up activities help students integrate cultural knowledge with their language skills.

Graphic literacy is the focus of **Get Graphic,** a feature that offers practice in reading charts, graphs, diagrams, and timelines—skills that are crucial in the workplace and for preparing for the GED. **Get Graphic** provides high-interest stimuli related to the unit topics and characters while it incorporates or recycles target language structures. A typical feature of this page is a follow-up activity in which learners develop their own simple graphs or charts and share them with partners or groups. The activities on this page help students learn to read, interpret, and use information in a graphic format.

Problem-solving and critical-thinking skills are developed further in **Issues and Answers**. This feature typically presents two opinions—often in direct opposition—in formats such as advice columns or letters to the editor. **Issues and Answers** contains short, humorous texts with views of U.S. life from a variety of perspectives, including those of immigrants and their "cultural advisors"—the experts who help to orient the newcomers as they bridge the gap between their native and adopted countries.

At the very end of each unit in Book 1 is the self-assessment activity **Think About Learning,** a final reflection task that asks students to evaluate the quality of their own learning on the major content points, life skills, and language structures in the unit. In every even-numbered unit of Book 1, this activity follows **Wrap-Up,** a project requiring students to use a graphic organizer such as a T-chart, a Venn diagram, an idea map, or a timeline to brainstorm and organize ideas and then talk or write in a group. In odd-numbered units **Think About Learning** follows **Issues and Answers**. In each case, **Think About Learning** provides a way for students to assess what they have learned and provide feedback to the teacher, all of which helps to build a learner-centered classroom.

ABOUT BOOK 1

In Book 1 the unit format varies slightly from that of the other books in order to meet the special needs of beginners. Each Student Book unit is 10 pages long—more manageable than the 12 pages of each unit in Books 2–4. **Vocabulary Prompts** is significantly expanded to include illustrated clusters of vocabu-lary, such as foods, family relationships, and workers in the community. Also, **Sound Bites** occurs only once in each unit, and the pre-listening and post-listening tasks are reduced. These slight format differences make Book 1 easier for beginning students to handle and thus ensure their success.

ICONS

Contemporary English uses the following six icons throughout the series:

 Listening—All conversations and other speech samples are recorded on tape.

 Speaking—Students speak with a partner, a group, or the class.

 Reading—Students read a passage, a graphic, or a short text.

 Writing—Students write letters, words, or phrases.

 Critical Thinking—Students perform an activity that requires critical-thinking skills.

 Spotlight—Students complete an exercise that provides practice on the structures presented on the **Spotlight** page. These exercises may require a variety of language skills, but structure practice is the principal focus of the exercise.

SPOTLIGHT ON GREETINGS

Hi. I'm Ted Omachi.

Good afternoon, Mr. Omachi. One moment, please.

Ms. Robins, Mr. Omachi is here.

Hello, Ms. Robins. I'm Ted Omachi.

Good afternoon. Please sit down.

VOCABULARY PROMPTS

Talk about the words below.

Good morning.

Good afternoon.

Good evening.

Your Turn

Work in a group of 4. Greet each other. Say your name.

SPOTLIGHT ON THE ALPHABET

A B C D E F G H I J K L M N O P Q R S T U V W X Y Z

a b c d e f g h i j k l m n o p q r s t u v w x y z

Talk about the words below.

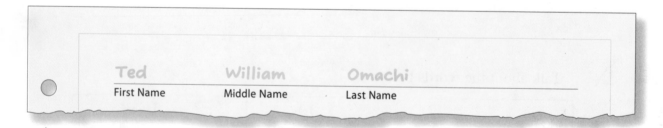

Ted	William	Omachi
First Name	Middle Name	Last Name

Your Turn

Work with a partner. Spell your first name. Spell your last name.

Talk about the words below.

773	555-2076
area code	phone number

Your Turn

Work with a partner. Read the phone numbers.
Then say your phone number.

1. 846-122-6779
2. 313-555-4023
3. 452-085-3474
4. 212-555-7845
5. 415-122-0931

SPOTLIGHT ON NUMBERS

10	11	12	13	14	15	16	17	18	19
ten	eleven	twelve	thirteen	fourteen	fifteen	sixteen	seventeen	eighteen	nineteen

20	31	42	53	64
twenty	thirty-one	forty-two	fifty-three	sixty-four

75	86	97	100	200
seventy-five	eighty-six	ninety-seven	one hundred	two hundred

And what's your address?

Three forty-six Bridge Street, Chicago, Illinois 60657.

VOCABULARY PROMPTS

Talk about the words below.

346 Bridge Street	Chicago	Illinois	60657
Address	City	State	Zip Code

Your Turn

Work with a partner. Read these addresses. Then say your address.

1. 38 Front Street, New York, New York 10001
2. 487 8th Street, Brownston, California 90054
3. 115 Glen Avenue, Stanton, California 90280
4. 230 Evans Road, Boston, Massachusetts 02108
5. 592 Bond Street, Austin, Texas 78701

SPOTLIGHT ON COMMANDS

Affirmative

Please sit down.

Spell your name.

Negative

Please don't smoke.

Don't write your name.

READING FOR REAL

Read Ted's form.

| Ted | William | Omachi | |
| First Name | Middle Name | Last Name | |

| 346 Bridge Street | Chicago | Illinois | 60657 |
| Address | City | State | Zip Code |

| 773 | 555-2076 |
| Area Code | Phone Number |

349-33-9956

Social Security Number

Your Turn

Write about you. Use a pen. Don't use a pencil.

| | | | |
| First Name | Middle Name | Last Name | |

| | | | |
| Address | City | State | Zip Code |

| | |
| Area Code | Phone Number |

Social Security Number

SPOTLIGHT ON TIME

 1:00
one o'clock

2:15
two fifteen
a quarter after two

3:30
three thirty
half past three

4:45
four forty-five
a quarter to five

Thank you, Ms. Robins. Good-bye.

Good-bye.

What time is it, Carmen?

It's five thirty.

Good night, Ms. Robins.

Good night, Carmen.

VOCABULARY PROMPTS

Talk about the words below.

five twenty-five
twenty-five after five

six forty
twenty to seven

seven ten
ten after seven

eight fifty-five
five to nine

  Your Turn

Work with a partner. Say the times. Then answer this question: What time is it now?

_____   _____   _____   _____

FRIENDS AND FAMILY

 SCENE 1

Talk about the pictures. Ask and answer the questions.

Ann and Rita work in a restaurant.
Ann is a waitress. Rita is a cook.
They have family photos.

Questions

Where is Ann's brother?
Where are Rita's brothers?

Do you have brothers?

1

VOCABULARY PROMPTS

With your teacher and other students, talk about the words below.

family photos   handsome   miss

mechanic

cook

student

waitress

mother   father

daughter/sister

sons/brothers

parents

children

 ## SOUND BITES

Exercise 1: Listen. Find the picture. Circle *a* or *b*.

1.
a.   b.

2.
a.   b.

3.
a.   b.

4.
a.   b.

 Your Turn

Listen again and repeat.

SPOTLIGHT ON SUBJECT PRONOUNS

I am from Texas.

We are from the United States.

He is from Vietnam.

She is from Thailand.

You are from Thailand.

You are from Asia.

It is from Peru.

They are from Asia.

Exercise 2: Look at the pictures. Complete the sentences.

1. ___He___ is from Asia. 2. _____ are from Europe. 3. _____ is from South America.

4. _____ is from Africa. 5. _____ are from North America. 6. _____ are from Australia.

Your Turn

Where are you from? Tell a partner. Complete the sentences.

YOU: _____ am from _____.

PARTNER: _____ is from _____.

SPOTLIGHT ON PRESENT TENSE OF *BE*

Complete Forms

I	**am**	a waitress.	Rita	**is**	a cook.	You	**are**	mechanics.
			He	**is**	a cook.	We	**are**	mechanics.
			She	**is**	a cook.	They	**are**	mechanics.
			It	**is**	a restaurant.			

Contractions

I'm	a waitress.	**Rita's**	a cook.	**You're**	mechanics.
		He's	a cook.	**We're**	mechanics.
		She's	a cook.	**They're**	mechanics.
		It's	a restaurant.		

An apostrophe (') means a letter is missing.

Exercise 3: Complete the sentences. Use *am, is,* or *are*.

1. Ann __is__ a waitress. She __is__ sad. She misses her brother.

2. Ann and I _____ in the United States now. We _____ students.

3. You and Ann _____ in a restaurant. You _____ happy.

4. My brother _____ in New York. He _____ a mechanic.

5. Rita's brothers _____ in Mexico. They _____ handsome.

Person to Person

Listen to the conversation. Practice it with a partner.

RITA: Hi. I'm Rita Vargas.
I'm from Mexico. I'm a cook.

CHAN: Hi, Rita. I'm Chan Luong.
I'm from Vietnam. I'm a student.

RITA: He's Pedro Flores. He's from Peru.
He's a mechanic.

Your Turn

Talk in groups of 3. Give your information.
Then introduce one student to the other student.

YOU: Hi. I'm _____. I'm from _____. I'm a _____.

She's / He's _____. She's / He's from _____. She's / He's a _____.

READING FOR REAL

THE MARTIN FAMILY

Adam Martin is a single parent.
His children want videos from
Home Cinema Movies.
Here is the application card.

Tina

Daniel

Linda

Adam

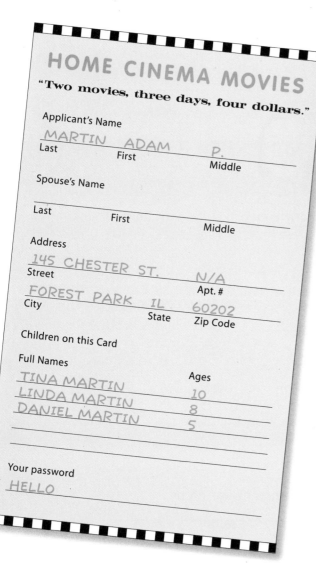

HOME CINEMA MOVIES
"Two movies, three days, four dollars."

Applicant's Name
MARTIN   ADAM   P.
Last   First   Middle

Spouse's Name

Last   First   Middle

Address
145 CHESTER ST.   N/A
Street   Apt. #
FOREST PARK   IL   60202
City   State   Zip Code

Children on this Card

Full Names
                        Ages
TINA MARTIN   10
LINDA MARTIN   8
DANIEL MARTIN   5

Your password
HELLO

 Exercise 4: What do you think?
Circle *yes*, *no*, or *not sure*.
With a partner compare answers.

1. Adam is the father of four children.

   yes   no   not sure

2. The Martin family is in New York.

   yes   no   not sure

3. The children are 5, 8, and 10 years old.

   yes   no   not sure

4. The card is for parents and children.

   yes   no   not sure

5. The password is *hello*.

   yes   no   not sure

6. The movies are a good price.
   yes   no   not sure

 Talk About It

Do you get videos at a good price?
Do you need a card and a password? Talk to a partner.
Tell about the price and the store.

CULTURE CORNER

Read about Chan Luong's family tree.

Chan Luong is from Vietnam.
He lives in San Diego now.
His wife, Kim, is American.
Chan's parents live with them.
Kim's parents are in New York.

Ming Luong   Hang Doan Luong

Thu Luong   Duc Luong   Hanh Luong   Chan Luong   Kim Young Luong

Exercise 5: Fill in the blanks.

1. _____ and _____ are Chan's parents.

2. _____, _____, and _____ are Chan's brothers and sisters.

3. _____ is Chan's wife.

4. Chan's parents live with Chan and Kim.   yes   no

5. Kim's parents live with Chan and Kim.   yes   no

Your Turn

Look at Chan's family tree. Write the names in the chart.

PARENTS	BROTHERS	SISTERS

In Your Experience

Talk to a partner. Do parents live with adult children in your country?
Make your family tree on a piece of paper. Write the names.
Then talk about your family tree. Use *am, is,* and *are.*

SCENE 2

Talk about the pictures. Ask and answer the questions.

Ann and Rita have photos of their parents.

My mother and father are from New York. They're retired now.

My mother is from Mexico. My father is from Texas.

They're not retired. They're teachers.

Questions

Where are Ann's parents from?

Where is Rita's mother from?

Where is her father from?

Where are your parents from?

V O C A B U L A R Y   P R O M P T S

With your teacher and other students, talk about the words below.

friend   retired

construction worker

teacher

restaurant

school

Marital Status   single   married   divorced   widowed

SPOTLIGHT ON PRESENT TENSE OF *BE* WITH THE NEGATIVE

I **am not**	retired.	Ana **is not**	retired.	We **are not**	retired.
I**'m not**	retired.	Ana**'s not**	retired.	We**'re not**	retired.
		She **is not**	retired.	You **are not**	retired.
		She**'s not**	retired.	You**'re not**	retired.
		He **is not**	retired.	They **are not**	retired.
		He**'s not**	retired.	They**'re not**	retired.
		It **is not**	a school.		
		It**'s not**	a school.		

She**'s not** = She **isn't**   They**'re not** = They **aren't**

 Exercise 6: Circle the correct choice.

1. He's a construction worker. He *(is not / am not)* a mechanic.

2. You're a student. You *(is not / are not)* a teacher.

3. They're teachers. They *(am not / are not)* retired.

4. She's a waitress. She *(is not / are not)* a cook.

5. My wife and I are retired. We *(are not / is not)* construction workers.

6. It's a school. It *(am not / is not)* a restaurant.

  Person to Person

Listen to the conversation. Then practice it with a partner.

RITA: Hi, Chan. I'm Rita Vargas.
         I'm a cook in a restaurant.
         And I'm a student in a school.

CHAN: You're a cook in a school?

RITA: Oh, no, Chan. I'm not a cook in a school.
         I'm a student in a school.
         I'm a cook in a restaurant!

   Your Turn

Look at the conversation again. Write a conversation with a partner.
Use your information. Use contractions.

GET GRAPHIC

There are 150 students at Brown Adult School.
The students are single, married, divorced,
or widowed. Look at the pie graph.

PIE GRAPH: STUDENTS AT
BROWN ADULT SCHOOL

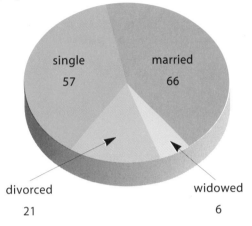

Exercise 7: Match the statements with the correct numbers.
Say the statements to a partner.

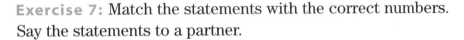

STATEMENT		NUMBER
1. _66_ students are married.		21
2. _____ students are not married.		66
3. _____ students are divorced.		144
4. _____ students are widowed.		84
5. _____ students are not widowed.		6

  In Your Experience

 Write information about you. Use *am* or *am not.*
Then share your answers with other students.

I _____ from the United States. I _____ married.

I _____ a parent. I _____ a father. I _____ a mother.

I _____ a son. I _____ a daughter.

I _____ a sister. I _____ a brother.

I _____ a student.

ISSUES AND ANSWERS

Read the letters.

 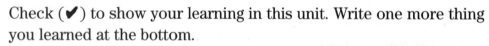 

Ask ABDUL and ANITA

DEAR ANITA,

I am from Latin America. My parents are retired. They live with me now.

I have three American friends. Their parents are retired, but they are not with their children. Why do many American parents and adult children live in different homes?

CURIOUS

DEAR CURIOUS,

You are right. In the United States some retired parents live with their children. But many retired parents live in different homes.

Why? Many adult children have jobs in different cities. Many parents don't want to live with their children. They want to be alone.

ANITA

What do you think about the issue and the answer?
Are there other answers? Talk with two students.
Tell you what you think.

Think About Learning

Check (✔) to show your learning in this unit. Write one more thing you learned at the bottom.

SKILLS / STRUCTURES	Page	easy ☺	so-so ☺	difficult ☹
Read an application	5			
Make a family tree	6			
Write a conversation	8			
Read a pie chart	9			
Tell what you think	10			
Use subject pronouns	3			
Use the present tense of *be* (statements)	4			
Use the present tense of *be* (negatives)	8			

PEOPLE IN THE WORKPLACE

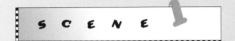

Talk about the pictures. Ask and answer the questions.

Hoa wants a job. He needs an application.
He looks for the manager's office in a hotel.

Questions

What does Hoa need?
Who does Hoa need to see?

Do you have a job?

With your teacher and other students, talk about the words below.

job application   busy   office

Hotel Employees

clerk   cashier   housekeeper

Your words

groundskeeper   manager   _____

SOUND BITES

Exercise 1: Listen. Find the picture. Circle *a* or *b*.

1.

a.   b.

2.

a.   b.

3.

a.   b.

4.

a.   b.

      Your Turn

Listen again and repeat.

Yes / No Questions

Statement: **He is** the manager.   **You are** a clerk.

Question: **Is he** the manager?   **Are you** a clerk?

In a question, the verb *be (am, is, are)* is first.

Short Answers

	Affirmative	**Negative**
Question:	**Is Hoa** Vietnamese?	**Is Hoa** a manager?
Short Answer:	**Yes, he is.**	**No, he's not.** OR **No, he isn't.**
Question:	**Are they** busy?	**Are they** clerks?
Short Answer:	**Yes, they are.**	**No, they're not.** OR **No, they aren't.**

Exercise 2: Read the story about the hotel employees. Then write a question for each answer below.

The Hillsun is a busy hotel. Don and Pam are clerks. Marie is a cashier. Ben is a groundskeeper. Ms. Bates is the manager.

1. *(Don and Pam)* _____Are_____ _____they_____ clerks?
   Yes, they are. They are clerks.

2. *(Marie)* _____ _____ a cashier?
   Yes, she is. She is a cashier.

3. *(Marie)* _____ _____ the manager?
   No, she isn't. She is not the manager.

4. *(Ben)* _____ _____ a groundskeeper?
   Yes, he is. He is a groundskeeper.

Exercise 3: In your notebook copy the questions from Exercise 2.
Write a *yes* answer for question 3.
Write *no* answers for questions 1, 2, and 4.

SPOTLIGHT ON SINGULAR AND PLURAL NOUNS

Singular (one)	Plural (two or more)
a student	students
a busy clerk	busy clerks
an office	offices
She is **a housekeeper.**	They are managers.

Add -s for the plural.

Irregular nouns are different:

child–child**ren**

man–m**e**n

woman–wom**e**n

Use *an* before *a, e, i, o,* or *u*. Do not use *a* or *an* with plural nouns.

Exercise 4: Write questions and short answers about the hotel employees.

1. *(manager)* Is he ____a manager____ ?

   No, ____he isn't____ .

2. *(housekeeper)* Are they _____ ? Yes, _____ .

3. *(cashier)* Are they _____ ? No, _____ .

4. *(groundskeeper)* Is he a _____ ? Yes, _____ .

5. *(busy hotel)* Is it a _____ ? Yes, _____ .

Person to Person

Listen to the conversation. Then practice it with a partner.

HOA: Excuse me. Are you the manager?

MAN: No, I'm not. I'm a clerk. Can I help you?

Your Turn

Talk with a partner. Ask a yes / no question about jobs. Then tell what your job is.

YOU: Are you a _____ ?

PARTNER: No, I'm not. I'm a _____ .

With your teacher and other students, talk about the words below.

experience   computers   day or night   good   fill out

READING FOR REAL

MARIE FRANK

Marie Frank is a hotel cashier.
But she wants a new job. So she fills out
job applications. And she has a mini-résumé.
The mini-résumé is a card. It tells what
she can do. She gives the mini-résumé
to friends, clerks, managers,
and hotel cashiers.

MARIE FRANK
HOME: (303) 555 -1278
JOB: Hotel Cashier

✓ 7 years of experience
✓ Uses computers
✓ Good with people
✓ Can work day or night

Exercise 5: Think about the
mini-résumé. Circle *yes*, *no*,
or *not sure*. Compare answers.

1. Marie is retired.

   yes   (no)   not sure

2. Marie has experience.

   yes   no   not sure

3. She is good with people.

   yes   no   not sure

4. She has a mini-application.

   yes   no   not sure

5. Marie fills out a mini-résumé.

   yes   no   not sure

Talk About It

Talk in a group. Talk about these questions:
Do you or your friends fill out job applications?
Can a mini-résumé help you get a job?

With your teacher and other students, talk about the words below.

supervisor   laundry worker   waiter / waitress   front desk   maintenance

CULTURE CORNER

A supervisor tells workers what to do. Look at the chart.
Who are the supervisors at the Hillsun Hotel?

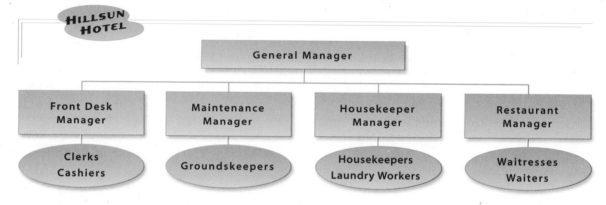

Exercise 6: Answer the questions, with a partner.

1. Is the restaurant manager a supervisor?
2. Are the cashiers supervisors?
3. Are the housekeepers supervisors?

Your Turn

In a group write a hotel job for each student. Ask, "Do you have experience?"

STUDENT NAME	JOB IN THE HOTEL	EXPERIENCE?	
		yes	no
		yes	no
		yes	no
		yes	no

In Your Experience

Think about your workplace or a friend's workplace. Then make a chart
on a large piece of paper. Show who the supervisors are. Show the jobs
at your workplace. Then share your chart with other students.

SCENE 2

Talk about the pictures. Ask and answer the questions.

Hoa's talking to the manager at the hotel. He has a job application.

I'm a good groundskeeper. This is my application.

JOB OPENINGS
• WAITRESS
• HOUSEKEEPER
• GROUNDSKEEPER

MANAGER

Oh, good! The hotel needs 2 new groundskeepers.

MANAGER

JOB OPENINGS
• WAITRESS
• HOUSEKEEPER
• GROUNDSKEEPER

Questions

Is Hoa a groundskeeper?
Does the hotel need a groundskeeper?

Do you work in a hotel?

V O C A B U L A R Y   P R O M P T S

With your teacher and other students, talk about the words below.

near   far   good   job openings   new

Workplaces

hotel

restaurant

factory

hospital

store

Your words

_____

SPOTLIGHT ON DEMONSTRATIVE PRONOUNS

	Singular	**Plural**
Near	**This** is a notebook.	**These** are notebooks.
Far	**That** is a notebook.	**Those** are notebooks.

Use *this* and *these* when something is near.
Use *that* and *those* when something is far.
Contraction: *that is = that's*

Exercise 7: Circle the correct answers.

1. (This is a book.)   That's a book.   2. This is a notebook.   That's a notebook.

3. These are pencils.   Those are pencils.   4. These are chairs.   Those are chairs.

Person to Person

Listen to the conversation. Then practice it with a partner.

CLERK: What are those?

CASHIER: These? These are new pencils. Do you want one?

CLERK: Yes, please.

Your Turn

Study the conversation. With a partner write a new conversation
in your notebook. Use *this*, *that*, *these*, and *those*. Then share
your conversation with the class.

With your teacher and other students, talk about the words below.

places   buy   things   services

GET GRAPHIC

The United States has many stores and restaurants. Look at the Top Five list.

TOP FIVE PLACES TO BUY THINGS IN THE UNITED STATES

	PLACE	NUMBER IN THE UNITED STATES
	1. Places to eat and drink	409,836
	2. Places to buy cars and services	178,700
	3. Food stores	168,272
	4. Clothes and shoe stores	121,283
	5. Furniture stores	106,441

Exercise 8: Write the correct letters from Column B in the sentences in Column A.

COLUMN A

1. You can buy cars and services at _____ places.

2. Restaurants are _____ .

3. You can buy chairs at _____ stores.

4. You can buy _____ at 121,283 stores.

COLUMN B

a. places to eat and drink

b. 178,700

c. clothes and shoes

d. 106,441

In Your Experience

Are there many stores, restaurants, and other places to work where you live? In a group list the top five places where people work.

WRAP-UP

Work in a group of 3. Ask the yes/no questions below. Give short answers.
Write yes or no on the chart. Share your chart with other students.

QUESTIONS	ANSWERS		
	Student Name	Student Name	Student Name
1. Are you a restaurant worker?			
2. Are you a factory worker?			
3. Are you a hotel worker?			
4. Are you a store clerk?			
5. Are you a worker?			

Think About Learning

Check (✔) to show your learning in this unit.
Write one more thing at the bottom.

SKILLS / STRUCTURES	Page	easy ☺	so-so 😐	difficult ☹
Read a mini-résumé	15			
Talk about workplace supervisors	16			
Read a "Top Five" list	19			
Make a group chart	20			
Use present of *be* in yes/no questions and short answers	13			
Use singular and plural nouns	14			
Use demonstrative pronouns	18			

HELPERS IN THE COMMUNITY

SCENE 1

Talk about the pictures. Ask and answer the questions.

Sue and Carla are talking about drugs in the schools.

Questions

Who is worried?
Why is she worried?

Do you have children?
Are you worried about your children?

VOCABULARY PROMPTS

With your teacher and other students, talk about the words below.

worried   drug   know   read   school

Community Helpers

principal

volunteer

police officer

counselor

doctor

Your words

_____

SOUND BITES

Exercise 1: Listen. Find the picture. Circle *a* or *b*.

1.

(a.)   b.

2.

a.   b.

a.   b.

4.

a.   b.

   Your Turn

Listen again and repeat.

SPOTLIGHT ON POSSESSIVE ADJECTIVES

Subject Pronouns	Possessive Adjectives	Possessive + Noun
I	**my**	**my** name
you	**your**	**your** name
he	**his**	**his** name
she	**her**	**her** name
it	**its**	**its** name
we	**our**	**our** name
they	**their**	**their** name

Exercise 2: Complete the sentences about Sue and Carla.
Use possessive adjectives.

1. *(She)* ___Her___ friend is worried.

2. *(I)* _____ son is OK.

3. *(We)* _____ children go to school.

4. *(They)* _____ school has a principal.

5. *(He)* _____ name is Mr. Lee.

Person to Person

Listen to the conversation. Then practice it with a partner.

LUC: I need more English for my job.
Tell me about your school for adults.

DAN: Oh, our school is a busy place. Our classes are good.
My teacher helps me. I like my class!

Your Turn

Study the conversation. With a partner tell about your school,
teacher, and class. Use possessive adjectives.

In Your Experience

Work in groups of 3. Talk about a friend.
Tell about his or her family or job.
Use possessive adjectives.

SPOTLIGHT ON PREPOSITIONS OF PLACE

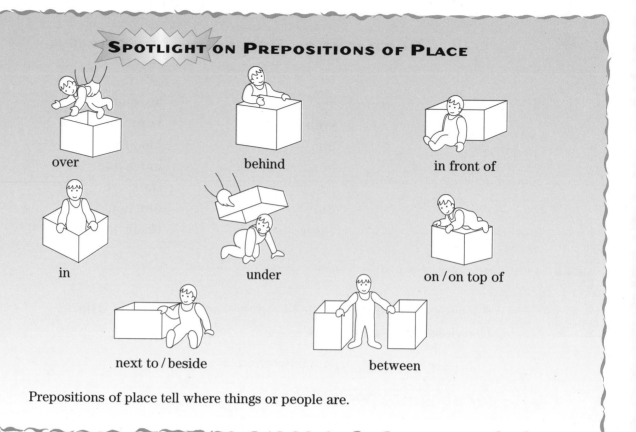

over

behind

in front of

in

under

on / on top of

next to / beside

between

Prepositions of place tell where things or people are.

Exercise 3: Complete the sentences. Use the prepositions of place.

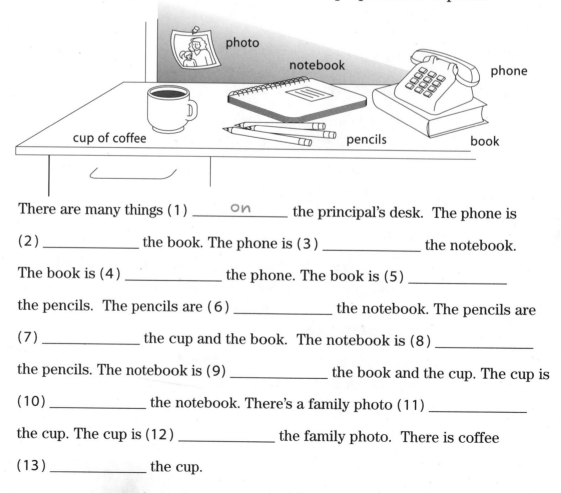

photo

notebook

phone

cup of coffee

pencils

book

There are many things (1) _____on_____ the principal's desk. The phone is

(2) _____ the book. The phone is (3) _____ the notebook.

The book is (4) _____ the phone. The book is (5) _____

the pencils. The pencils are (6) _____ the notebook. The pencils are

(7) _____ the cup and the book. The notebook is (8) _____

the pencils. The notebook is (9) _____ the book and the cup. The cup is

(10) _____ the notebook. There's a family photo (11) _____

the cup. The cup is (12) _____ the family photo. There is coffee

(13) _____ the cup.

Talk about the words with your teacher and other students.

meetings   problems   crime   department

READING FOR REAL

The school has meetings for parents. Read the meeting schedule.

OUR CHILDREN AND THEIR PROBLEMS

Mondays in September, 7:00 - 9:00 P.M.
Lincoln School Cafeteria

Sept. 1   **NO DRUGS IN MY SCHOOL!**
Mr. Daniel Lee, school principal

Sept. 8   **Your Children and Their Doctor**
Dr. Rani Chaaptar, children's doctor

Sept. 15   **Crime in Our Cities**
Officer Paul Ortega, Police Department

Sept. 22   **Talk with Your Child**
Ms. Alicia Newton, counselor

Exercise 4: What do you think?
Circle *yes*, *no*, or *not sure*.

1. The classes are on Tuesdays.

   yes   (no)   not sure

2. There are 9 meetings.

   yes   no   not sure

3. Daniel Lee is a school principal.

   yes   no   not sure

4. Parents talk about children's problems.

   yes   no   not sure

5. Dr. Chaaptar talks about crime.

   yes   no   not sure

Talk About It

Talk to a partner. Talk about these questions:
Are drugs are a problem in the schools?
Can principals, doctors, counselors, and police help? How?

With your teacher and other students, talk about the words below.

kind   products   make   give

CULTURE CORNER

Communities have many different kinds of workers. Some workers make products or give services. Other workers help people in the community with their needs or problems.

Your Turn

Look at the jobs below. Write the jobs in the correct columns in the chart.

teacher	volunteer	office clerk	doctor
groundskeeper	video store cashier	police officer	factory worker
school principal	hotel manager	drug counselor	waitress

FACTORY OR SERVICE JOBS	COMMUNITY HELPERS
groundskeeper	teacher

In Your Experience

List the community helpers you know.
Do you want to be a community helper?
Check (✔) the job(s) you want in the chart above,
or write the name of a different job you want.
Share your list with other students.

S C E N E **2**

Talk about the pictures. Ask and answer the questions.

Carla is at the school. She's talking to the principal. She's asking for help.

Questions

Where is Carla?

When are the classes for parents?

Do you know a school principal?

V O C A B U L A R Y   P R O M P T S

With your teacher and other students, talk about the words below.

come in   sit down   teach

Schools   class   gym   cafeteria

classroom   auditorium   Your words

_____

SPOTLIGHT ON *A* AND *AN*

a classroom   **a** gym

A and *an* mean *one*. Use *a* before most words—words beginning with consonant sounds.

an auditorium   **an** office   **an** exit

Use *an* before words that begin with vowel sounds. *A, e, i, o* and *u* are vowels.

Exercise 5: Jane's daughter, Sara, is learning to talk. Sara asks a lot of questions about words and things. Complete the conversations. For each answer use *a* or *an* with a noun.

1.

SARA: What's that?

JANE: That's _____.

2.

SARA: What's this?

JANE: This is _____.

3.

SARA: What's this?

JANE: This is _____.

4.

SARA: What's that?

JANE: That's _____.

5.

SARA: What's this?

JANE: This is _____.

6.

SARA: What's that?

JANE: That's _____.

With your teacher and other students, talk about the words below.

bad   cigarettes   drinks   beer   month

 GET GRAPHIC

Many community helpers tell us, "Don't use drugs!" They don't want drugs in our cities or our homes. But some products in stores are drugs! The *alcohol* in beer is a drug. The *nicotine* in cigarettes is a drug. The *caffeine* in coffee and other drinks is a drug. Are these drugs a problem in the United States? Look at the bar graph.

ALCOHOL, NICOTINE, AND CAFFEINE USERS IN THE UNITED STATES

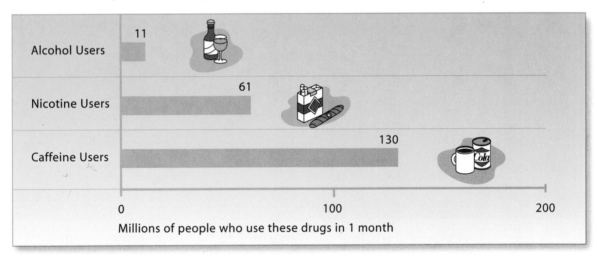

Millions of people who use these drugs in 1 month

 Exercise 6: Write the correct numbers from Column B in the sentences in Column A.

COLUMN A	COLUMN B
1. _____ million people use alcohol.	61
2. _____ million people use caffeine.	1
3. _____ million people use nicotine.	11
4. 11,000,000 people use alcohol in _____ month.	130

 In Your Experience

Talk in a group. Are alcohol, nicotine, and caffeine bad for people? Why or why not?

ISSUES AND ANSWERS

Read the letters.

Ask ABDUL and ANITA

DEAR ABDUL,

My brother has a problem with alcohol. He drinks beer with his friends at night. I'm worried about his family. His wife is worried about his job. His children need their father at home. Please tell me how to help my brother.

HELP

DEAR HELP,

Alcohol is a problem because it is a drug. Your brother needs help. Call a community group or counselor. Ask about their services. Talk with your brother. Listen. Tell him you are worried. Tell him about the services he can use.

ABDUL

Talk with other students about the letter and the answer.
Is the answer good or bad?

Think About Learning

Check (✔) to show your learning in this unit. Write one more thing at the bottom.

SKILLS / STRUCTURES	Page	easy ☺	so-so ☺	difficult ☹
Read a schedule	25			
Make a chart	26			
Read a bar graph	29			
Read and talk about problems	25			
Use possessive adjectives	23			
Use prepositions of place	24			

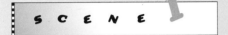

Talk about the pictures. Ask and answer the questions.

Mark is asking his neighbor for help.

Questions

What does Mark need?
What is Jenny doing today?

Do you have children?

With your teacher and other students, talk about the words below.

vacation   babysitter   sick   sorry

Neighbors
Helping
Neighbors

babysitting

getting the newspaper

checking the mail

watching the house

taking care of the pets

Your words

_____

SOUND BITES

Exercise 1: Listen. Find the picture. Circle *a* or *b*.

1.

a.   b.   a.   b.

3.   4.

a.   b.   a.   b.

  Your Turn

Listen again and repeat.

SPOTLIGHT ON PRESENT CONTINUOUS AFFIRMATIVE STATEMENTS

am	is	are
I **am working.**	Mark **is working.**	We **are working.**
	He	
	She	
	It	

Use *am*, *is*, or *are* + verb + *-ing* to tell about an action happening right now or in the near future.

Note the spelling: mak**e**–mak**ing**   us**e**–us**ing**   get–get**ting**

Contractions: **I'm/You're/He's/She's/We're/They're** working.

Exercise 2: Kamal is on vacation. What is he doing?
Work with a partner. Talk about the pictures.
For example, say, "He's watching TV."

watch TV

talk to a friend

drink coffee

look at photos

read the newspaper

call a neighbor

Exercise 3: In your notebook write sentences about Kamal.
For example, write, "He's watching TV."

SPOTLIGHT ON NEGATIVE STATEMENTS IN THE PRESENT CONTINUOUS

am	is	are
I **am not working.**	Jenny **is not working.**	We **are not working.**
	She	They
	He	
	It	

Use *not* after *am, is,* or *are* to make a negative statement.

Contractions: **I'm/You're/He's/She's/We're/They're** not working.

Exercise 4: Glen and Sandy are hotel clerks. But they are not working now. Write the sentences below in the negative.

1. Glen is working today. He's using a computer.

   Glen isn't working today. He's not using a computer.

2. Sandy is working at the desk. She's opening mail.

   _____

3. Glen and Sandy are going to a meeting.

   _____

4. They're taking care of people. They're talking.

   _____

Exercise 5: Look at the pictures in Exercise 2 on page 33. Kamal isn't doing those things now. Now Kamal is working again. In your notebook write sentences in the negative. For example, write, "He's not watching TV now."

  Person to Person

Listen to the conversation. Then practice it with a partner.

RAUL: I'm not working now.

JEAN: What are you doing?

RAUL: I'm studying English. But I'm not reading my book. I'm writing sentences.

  Your Turn

Study the conversation. Talk with a partner. Tell what you're doing now. Use the present continuous.

With your teacher and other students, talk about the words below.

child-care center   fee   per week   expensive   average

READING FOR REAL

In the United States there are 100,000 child-care centers.
They take care of children. The fees are different in many cities.
Look at the chart. It shows the fees for May 1, 1996.

CHILD-CARE FEES IN THE UNITED STATES

Average fee per week for children in child-care centers			
City	Age 1	Age 3	Age 6
Boston, Massachusetts	$228	$170	$128
Orlando, Florida	$83	$73	$38
Dallas, Texas	$89	$81	$51
Oakland, California	$145	$125	$70

Exercise 6: Think about the chart. Then circle *yes, no,* or *not sure* for the questions below.

1. Child care is expensive in Boston.

   (yes)   no   not sure

2. Child care for children age 1 is expensive.

   yes   no   not sure

3. The fees are for one month.

   yes   no   not sure

4. The fees are for a babysitter at home.

   yes   no   not sure

5. In Dallas it's $51 per week for a child age 6.

   yes   no   not sure

Talk About It

How much is child care in your community?
In your opinion, why is child care expensive?

With your teacher and other students, talk about the words below.

house   apartment   important   advice   boss

CULTURE CORNER

People are busy in the United States.
They work hard and take care
of families. Many people don't
know their neighbors.
But neighbors are important.
Neighbors can help.
Here is advice from the
Police Department:

ARE YOU GOING ON VACATION?

Ask a neighbor to take care of your home.
For example, ask your
neighbor to do these things:

✓ watch your house
(or apartment)

✓ check your mail

✓ get your newspaper

✓ call the police
about problems

Do these things for your neighbors too!

Your Turn

Look at the list of services.
Check (✔) the things you ask your neighbor to do
when you're on vacation. Mark an X for things you do for your neighbor.
Compare your list with a partner's list. Talk about the differences.

_____ babysit children   _____ watch the house

_____ check the mail   _____ do the laundry

_____ get the newspaper   _____ take care of pets

_____ take care of the car   _____ answer the phone

_____ take care of parents   _____ call teachers

_____ drive children to school   _____ call the boss at work

In Your Experience

Talk with other students. Tell about neighbors in your country.
What do they do for you? What do you do for your neighbors?

Talk about the pictures. Ask and answer the questions.

Mark, Rosa, and Jenny are neighbors. They are doing laundry.
They are talking about child care.

Are you looking for a babysitter? Try a child-care co-op!

A what?

A child-care co-op. Two or three neighbors take turns caring for children.

Questions

Who is reading about child-care co-ops?
What is a child-care co-op?

Do your friends or neighbors have a child-care co-op?

V O C A B U L A R Y   P R O M P T S

With your teacher and other students, talk about the words below.

co-op   take turns   try

Children's Activities

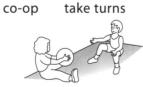

playing

sleeping

watching TV

eating

reading

Your words

_____

Statements

She **is working** today.

They **are working** today.

Yes/No Questions	**Short Answers**	
Is she **working** today?	Yes, **she is.**	No, **she's not.**
		No, **she's not.**
Are they **working** today?	Yes, **they are.**	No, **they're not.**
		No, **they aren't.**

Use *am, is,* or *are* before the subject to make questions about actions happening now.

Exercise 7: Complete the questions and short answers below.

1. Lee is working.

   <u>Is Lee working?</u> _____ Yes, _____ <u>she is</u> _____.

2. Her children are studying.

   _____ Yes, _____.

3. They aren't going on vacation.

   _____ No, _____.

4. Lee's sister is babysitting.

   _____ Yes, _____.

5. She is watching TV.

   _____ Yes, _____.

Your Turn

In your notebook write 6 questions with the verbs below.
With a partner take turns asking questions. Give short answers.
For example, ask, "Are you studying today, Kim?"
And answer, "Yes, I am."

studying	going	asking	helping	talking	reading
working	writing	drinking	telling	watching	babysitting

GET GRAPHIC

Some neighbors have a work schedule for their new child-care co-op. They take turns babysitting the children. Read their work schedule.

CHILD-CARE CO-OP WORK SCHEDULE 1

	Sunday	Monday	Tuesday	Wednesday	Thursday	Friday	Saturday
Mark		✔					✔
Rosa			✔		✔		
Jenny				✔		✔	

Exercise 8: Write the correct letters from Column B in the sentences in Column A.

COLUMN A

1. The schedule is for ___1___ week.

2. Rosa babysits _____ days.

3. The parents need child care _____ days per week.

4. _____ parents take turns babysitting.

COLUMN B

2

3

1

6

Your Turn

The child-care co-op needs a new schedule. Read the sentences below. Then check (✔) to make a new schedule. With a partner compare your new schedules.

Jenny wants to babysit on Tuesday and Wednesday.
Mark can babysit on Friday and Saturday.
Rosa needs to babysit on Monday and Thursday.

CHILD-CARE CO-OP WORK SCHEDULE 2

	Sunday	Monday	Tuesday	Wednesday	Thursday	Friday	Saturday
Mark							
Rosa							
Jenny							

In Your Experience

Work in a group of 3. On a large piece of paper, make a schedule for your group from Sunday to Saturday. Write your names. Write a *W* on days you work. Write an *S* on the days you come to school.

WRAP-UP

Work in a group of 3. Ask the yes/no questions below.
Give short answers. Write yes or no on the chart.
Share your chart with other students.

QUESTIONS	ANSWERS		
	Student's Name	Student's Name	Student's Name
1. Are you working?			
2. Are you studying English?			
3. Are you babysitting?			

Think About Learning

Check (✔) to show your learning in this unit. Write one more thing at the bottom.

SKILLS / STRUCTURES	Page	easy ☺	so-so ☺	difficult ☹
Read a fee chart	35			
Talk about neighbors' services	36			
Read co-op work schedule	39			
Make a work or study schedule	39			
Make a yes/no chart	40			
Use present continuous statements (affirmative)	33			
Use present continuous statements (negative)	34			
Use present continuous yes/no questions and short answers	38			

EATING HEALTHY FOOD

SCENE 1

Talk about the pictures. Ask and answer the questions.

Ted and Ava are in a restaurant. But they aren't ready to order.

Questions

Are they ready to order?
What does Ted like? What doesn't Ava like?

What do you order
in a restaurant?

V O C A B U L A R Y   P R O M P T S

With your teacher and other students, talk about the words below.

ready   order   healthy   cook

Food

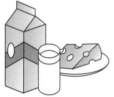

chicken / beef / fish

bread / rice

Your words

fruits

vegetables

milk / cheese

SOUND BITES

Exercise 1: Listen. Find the picture. Circle *a* or *b*.

1.

a.   b.

2.

a.   b.

3.

a.   b.

4.

a.   b.

 Your Turn

Listen again and repeat.

SPOTLIGHT ON SIMPLE PRESENT IN AFFIRMATIVE STATEMENTS

I	**like** beef.	He	**likes** beef.
You		She	
We		It	
They			

Use the simple present to talk about things that are always true or things that happen again and again. Remember to add *-s* or *-es* to the verb with *he*, *she*, or *it*.

Some verbs are irregular: I **have**
  He **has**

Exercise 2: Complete the story about Ted with the simple present.

Ted (1) *work* ____works____ in a food store. Ted (2) *know* _____

about healthy food. He (3) *eat* _____ beef, chicken, and fish.

He (4) *like* _____ to eat, and he (5) *try* _____ many foods.

Exercise 3: In your notebook change the sentences about Ted. Write sentences about Sam and Carmen. For example, write, "Sam and Carmen work in a food store."

Exercise 4: Write more sentences about you. Use *work*, *know*, *eat*, *like*, and *cook*. For example, write, "I cook healthy food."

Person to Person

Listen to the conversation. Then practice it with a partner.

WAITRESS: Are you ready to order?

MATTHEW: Yes. I want the beef with vegetables and rice. And a cup of coffee, please.

Your Turn

Study the conversation. Talk with a partner. Talk about the food and drinks you want to order in a restaurant.

In Your Experience

Talk with other students about the food you eat at home. Compare the food you buy with the food they buy. For example, say, "I buy rice and chicken. What do you buy?"

SPOTLIGHT ON SIMPLE PRESENT IN NEGATIVE STATEMENTS

I/You/We/They **do not like** fish.   He/She/It **does not like** fish.

don't   **doesn't**

Use *do not* or *does not* to make negative sentences with the simple present.

Don't add *-s* or *-es* to the main verb with *he*, *she*, or *it*.
Correct: *He doesn't eat fish.* Not correct: *He doesn't eats fish.*

Exercise 5: Complete the story about Lucy with verbs in the negative simple present.

Lucy (1) *eat* ___doesn't eat___ beef. She (2) *like* _____ fish.

Lucy (3) *order* _____ fruit in restaurants.

She (4) *cook* _____ well, and she (5) *buy* _____

good food.

Exercise 6: In your notebook write the sentences about Lucy and Bob again. For example, write, "Lucy and Bob don't eat beef."

Exercise 7: In your notebook write negative sentences about you. Use *eat*, *like*, *order*, *cook*, and *buy*. For example, write, "I don't eat chicken."

Exercise 8: Work with a partner. Rewrite the simple present verbs in the sentences below. Change affirmative to negative. Change negative to affirmative.

Ray and Pam (1) don't go to restaurants. They (2) *like* to eat at home.
(go) *(don't like)*

Pam (3) *cooks* well, but Ray (4) *doesn't want* to eat good food.

In restaurants Ray (5) *doesn't order* beef, fish, or chicken.

He (6) *drinks* milk. Pam (7) *doesn't eat* fruit or vegetables.

With your teacher and other students, talk about the words below.

servings   plan   sweets   fats   pasta

READING FOR REAL

Tom wants to eat healthy food.
So he looks at the food guide pyramid.
Then he plans his food for one day.

THE FOOD GUIDE PYRAMID

Sweets and Fats
(don't eat many)

Milk and Cheese
(eat 2–3 servings)

Chicken, Beef, and Fish
(eat 2–3 servings)

Vegetables
(eat 3–5 servings)

Fruits
(eat 3–5 servings)

Pasta, Bread, and Rice
(eat 6–11 servings)

Exercise 9: Think about the food pyramid. Circle *yes, no,*
or *not sure*. Then, with a partner compare your answers.

1. Tom can eat 2 apples.

   (yes)   no   not sure

2. Tom drinks 4 glasses of milk.

   yes   no   not sure

3. Tom can eat rice, pasta,
   and 4 pieces of bread.

   yes   no   not sure

4. Tom can eat 2 servings of vegetables.

   yes   no   not sure

5. Tom can eat many sweets and fats.

   yes   no   not sure

Talk About It

Do you eat healthy food? Compare your food with the food pyramid.
Talk about the food you eat in 1 day.

VOCABULARY PROMPTS

With your teacher and other students, talk about the words below.

fast food   grams   favorite   too much

CULTURE CORNER

People in the United States are very busy. So some Americans like to eat fast food. They eat in their favorite fast-food restaurants. Some fast food is healthy, but one problem is too much fat.

McDOE'S	
food	grams of fat
Beef Hamburger	9
Large French Fries	22
Cheeseburger	13
Chicken Nuggets	10
Apple Pie	15

ANDY'S	
food	grams of fat
Beef Sandwich	18
Fish Sandwich	27
Chicken Salad	7
Broccoli Soup	7

Your Turn

Write the name of the fast food in the correct group. Check (✔) the healthy foods. With a partner compare your answers.

0–9 grams of fat	10–17 grams of fat	18–27 grams of fat
Beef Hamburger		

In Your Experience

Talk about American fast food with other students. What fast-food restaurants do you like? What fast food do you eat? Does your favorite fast food have too much fat? Is your favorite fast food healthy?

S C E N E 2

Talk about the pictures. Ask and answer the questions.

Ted wants to go to the store. He's asking what Sam needs.

Questions

What does Sam need?
Does he want something healthy?

Do you eat healthy foods?
Which foods are healthy?

V O C A B U L A R Y   P R O M P T S

With your teacher and other students, talk about the words below.

unhealthy   sure   anything

More Food

cookies

butter

candy

potato chips

ice cream

Your words

_____

SPOTLIGHT ON SIMPLE PRESENT YES/NO QUESTIONS AND SHORT ANSWERS

Do	I	eat healthy food?	Yes,	I	do.	No,	I	don't
	you			you			you	
	we			we			we	
	they			they			they	
Does	he	eat healthy food?	Yes,	he	does.	No,	he	doesn't.
	she			she			she	
	it			it			it	

Use *do* or *does* + verb to make questions in the simple present.

Exercise 10: Write questions. Ask a partner the questions. Write the answers in your notebook.

1. (*you / like / beef*) Do you like beef? _____

2. (*Sam / eat / cookies*) _____

3. (*your friends / buy / too much candy*) _____

4. (*your family / cook / healthy food*) _____

5. (*you / drink / milk*) _____

Person to Person

Listen to the conversation. Then practice it with a partner.

MIMI: Do you eat sweets?

WALTER: No, I don't. I don't like them.

MIMI: Do you like potato chips?

WALTER: Yes, I sure do.

Your Turn

Study the conversation. Then talk with a partner. Ask questions about healthy and unhealthy food.

In Your Experience

In a group make a list of unhealthy foods. Check (✔) the foods with too much fat. Then share your list with other students.

With your teacher and other students, talk about the words below.

weight   height   pounds   overweight   feet (')   inches (")

GET GRAPHIC

Ted, Ava, and Sam want to be healthy. Check their weights on the chart.
Ted is 5'10" and 150 pounds. Ava is 5'2" and 115 pounds.
Sam is 6' and 200 pounds.

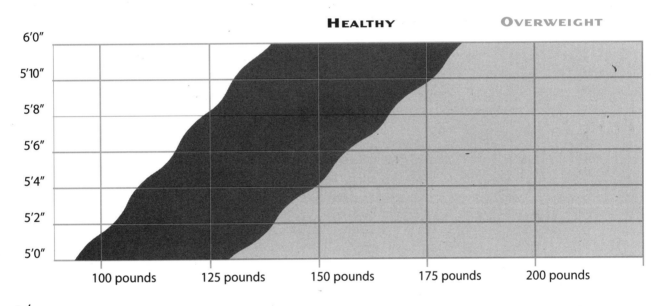

Exercise 11: Write the correct words from Column B
in the sentences in Column A.

COLUMN A

1. Sam is _____overweight_____ .

2. Ted's weight is _____ .

3. _____ have healthy weights.

4. Many Americans think being overweight is _____ .

COLUMN B

overweight

Ted and Ava

healthy

unhealthy

In Your Experience

Sam needs to eat healthy food for a healthy weight. In a group,
plan healthy food for Sam for 1 day. Write your plan on a large sheet
of paper. Then share your plan with the class.

ISSUES AND ANSWERS

Read the letters. Then talk with other students about the answer.
Is the answer good or bad?

 **Ask ABDUL and ANITA**

DEAR ANITA,

Sweets are unhealthy! Fast food is unhealthy! My favorite foods are unhealthy. I don't like eating healthy food. I'm not overweight. Can't I eat the foods I like?

CANDY

DEAR CANDY,

Years of eating sweets and fats can make you overweight. Too much fat can make you sick. Doctors know from experience. Listen to them. Make healthy foods your favorites!

ANITA

Think About Learning

Check (✔) to show your learning in this unit.
Write one more thing at the bottom.

SKILLS / STRUCTURES	Page	easy ☺	so-so ☹	difficult ☹
Read the food pyramid	45			
Talk about fast food	46			
Read a height and weight chart	49			
Plan healthy food for one day	49			
Use simple present in affirmative statements	43			
Use simple present in negative statements	44			
Use simple present in yes/no questions and short answers	48			

TRAVELING BY CAR

Talk about the pictures. Ask and answer the questions.

Bob and Fran are traveling by car with their children.
They're looking for the Dory Motel. It's 8:00 in the evening.

Questions

What's the motel exit number?
What time is it?

How do you travel?

VOCABULARY PROMPTS

With your teacher and other students, talk about the words below.

hard   snowing   cold   weather   temperature

Car Travel

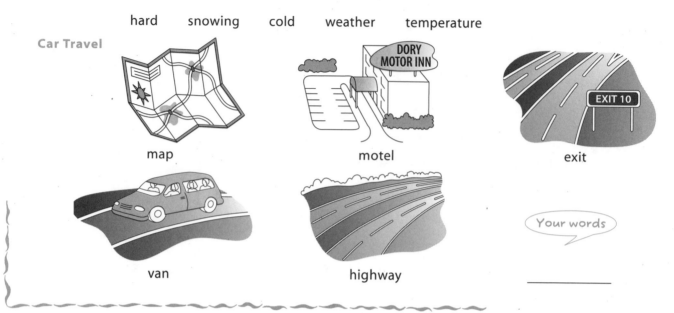

map

motel

exit

Your words

_____

van

highway

SOUND BITES

Exercise 1: Listen. Find the picture. Circle *a* or *b*.

1.
a.   b.

2.
a.   b.

3.
a.   b.

4.
a.   b.

  Your Turn

Listen again and repeat.

SPOTLIGHT ON INFORMATION QUESTIONS WITH *BE*

(person)	**Who**	is it?	**Who**	are they?
(thing)	**What**		**What**	
(hour)	**What time**			
(date/day)	**When**		**When**	
(place)	**Where**		**Where**	
(reason)	**Why**			
(distance)	**How far**		**How far**	
(quantity)	**How much**		**How much**	

To make an information question with *be*, put the wh-question word in front of a yes/no question.

Exercise 2: Maria's parents are on vacation. They are at a motel. Write an information question for each answer.

1.

Question: __What time is it?__
Answer: It's 10:30 A.M.

2.

Question: _____
Answer: It's in Florida.

3.

Question: _____
Answer: It's on June 21, 1999.

4.

Question: _____
Answer: They are Maria's parents.

Your Turn

Work with a partner. Write 5 information questions with *be*.
Ask other students your questions.

SPOTLIGHT ON INTRODUCTORY *It*

It's snowing!

It's = It is

It's 32 degrees.

BANK OF

It's 10 o'clock.

BANK OF

Use *It's* to talk about the weather, the temperature, and the time (clock time, days, months, and years).

More examples: **It's (It is)** Monday today. **It's (It is)** October. **It's (It is)** 1999.

Exercise 3: Work with a partner. Talk about the pictures below. Make sentences with *It's*. For example, say, "It's Sunday. It's April 12. It's raining."

1.

Sun. / Apr. 12 / raining

2.

Wed. / Mar. 15 / windy

3.

Fri. / Oct. 2 / cloudy

4.

Tues. / Dec. 22 / cold

5.

Thurs. / Aug. 4 / hot

6.
Sat. / Feb. 28 / snowing

Your Turn

Talk with a partner about the day, the date, and the weather today.

In Your Experience

In your notebook write about the weather for 7 days. Write days and dates too. For example, write, "It's Monday. It's October 16. It's windy and cold." With a partner compare your sentences.

With your teacher and other students, talk about the words below.

north   south   east   west   road

READING FOR REAL

Fran and Bob have a map to the motel. The Dory Motor Inn is on Orange Road and Front Street. Fran's reading the map.

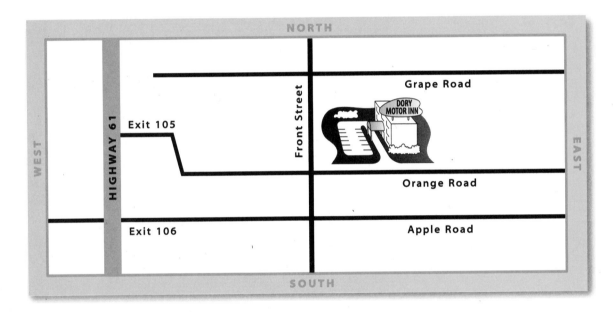

Exercise 4: Think about the map. Circle *yes, no,* or *not sure.* With a partner compare your answers.

1. The motel is on Orange Road.

   (yes)   no   not sure

2. Apple Road is south of Orange Road.

   yes   no   not sure

3. Take exit 106 to the motel.

   yes   no   not sure

4. Exit 110 is Apple Road.

   yes   no   not sure

5. Highway 61 is east of the motel.

   yes   no   not sure

Talk About It

Do you use maps? When? How does a map help you?

With your teacher and other students, talk about the words below.

love   dark   light   medium   truck

CULTURE CORNER

Americans love cars! There are about 146,400,000 cars in the United States.
To many people a car isn't only for travel. It's a friend or even one of the family.
Read the list of favorite car colors in the United States in 1995.

FAVORITE COLORS OF CARS	PERCENTAGE OF CARS IN THE UNITED STATES
black	9%
dark green	15%
light brown	8%
medium red	10%
white	18%

Exercise 5: Write the top 5 favorite colors of cars.
Then, with a partner compare your lists.

TOP FIVE FAVORITE COLORS OF CARS	PERCENTAGE OF CARS IN THE UNITED STATES
1. white	18%
2.	
3.	
4.	
5.	

In Your Experience

Work with your teacher. Ask these questions:
Do you have a car, a truck, or a van? What color is it?
What's your favorite color for a car? Make a list of the top 5
favorite colors of cars of the students in the class.

Talk about the pictures. Ask and answer the questions.

Bob and Fran are having car problems. Bob's talking to a mechanic.

Questions

What does Bob need?
What are Bob and the mechanic
talking about?

When do people need mechanics?

VOCABULARY PROMPTS

With your teacher and other students, talk about the words below.

only   old   cost   sir   sport-utility vehicle   test-drive

Car Maintenance

battery

oil

gas

tire

mechanic

Your words

_____

Who	**do**	I	**pay?**		Who	**does**	he	**pay?**
What		you			What		she	
When		we			When			
Where		they			Where			
Why					Why			
How much					How much			
How long					How long			

Use *do* or *does* with the verb to make information questions in the simple present.

In questions, *do/does* comes before the subject.

Exercise 6: Help Bob make questions about his car problems.

1. (*what/does/need*)

    <u>What</u> <u>does</u> the car <u>need</u> ?

2. (*how much/does/cost*)

    _____ _____ a new battery _____ ?

3. (*when/does/work*)

    _____ _____ the mechanic _____ ?

4. (*why/does/need*)

    _____ _____ the car _____ a battery?

Your Turn

In your notebook write 1 more question Bob can ask. Then write 3 questions you can ask a mechanic about a problem with your tires.

Person to Person

Listen to the conversation. Then practice it with a partner.

LILY: I love that red car. How much does it cost?

SALESMAN: The red car? It costs $50,000. Do you want to test-drive it?

LILY: What? $50,000? No, thank you! It's too expensive.

Your Turn

Study the conversation. Then, with a partner write another conversation about a new, dark green sport-utility vehicle. It costs $32,000.

With your teacher and other students, talk about the words below.

insurance   license   expenses   maintenance

GET GRAPHIC

Bob and Fran have a 1990 van. They take good care of their van.
The pie graph shows their car expenses for 1998.

1998 CAR EXPENSES $1,600.00

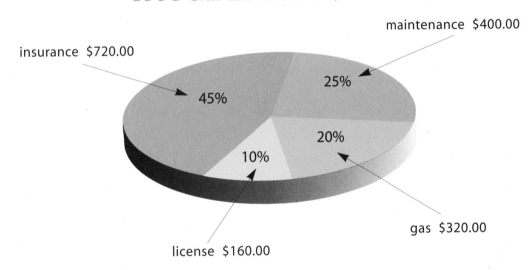

maintenance $400.00

insurance $720.00

45%

25%

20%

10%

gas $320.00

license $160.00

Exercise 7: Write the numbers from Column B in the
sentences in Column A.

COLUMN A	COLUMN B
1. The car expenses for 1998 are $ __1,600.00__ .	400.00
2. $ _____ is for maintenance.	25
3. $400.00 is _____ % of $1,600.00.	20
4. Gas costs _____ % of expenses per year.	1,600.00

In Your Experience

Bob and Fran's car maintenance costs $400.00 per year.
What kind of maintenance does a car need? Make a list with a partner.
With other students compare your lists.

WRAP-UP

In a group make an idea map. Write questions you can ask when you buy a car, a truck, a van, or a sport-utility vehicle. Share your questions with other students.

QUESTIONS TO ASK WHEN YOU BUY A CAR

How much does the insurance cost?

Think About Learning

Check (✔) to show your learning in this unit. Write one more thing at the bottom.

SKILLS / STRUCTURES	Page	easy ☺	so-so 😐	difficult ☹
Read a map	55			
Make a "top five" list with percentages	56			
Read a pie chart with percentages	59			
List car-maintenance needs	59			
Make an idea map	60			
Make information questions with *be*	53			
Use introductory *It*	54			
Make information questions with the simple present	58			

ASKING FOR A RAISE

Talk about the pictures. Ask and answer the questions.

Carl and Molly are talking about money problems.
They have a lot of bills.

Questions

Where does Carl work?
What's his job?

Do you want to ask for a raise?
Can you? Why or why not?

With your teacher and other students, talk about the words below.

bills   raise   after   just   customers

Office Work

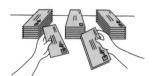

sort mail   type   answer phones

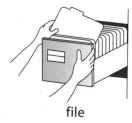

file   fax   Your words

_____

SOUND BITES

Exercise 1: Listen. Find the picture. Circle *a* or *b*.

1.

a.   b.

2.

a.   b.

3.

a.   b.

4.

a.   b.

     Your Turn

Listen again and repeat.

SPOTLIGHT ON *CAN* IN AFFIRMATIVE AND NEGATIVE STATEMENTS

Affirmative Statements

I / You / He / She / It / We / They   **can** type.

Negative Statements

I / You / He / She / It / We / They   **cannot (can't)** type.

Use *can* in 3 ways: I **can** type. (ability)

                            Can I go now? (permission)

                            Can you help me? (request)

 Exercise 2: Read the story.

Silvia works in an office.
She can do many things. She **types.**
She **answers the phone.**
She **talks with customers** about
their problems. Silvia needs help
with some things. She doesn't
file or **fax**.

 Exercise 3: Work with a partner. Complete the story.
Tell what Silvia *can* and *can't* do.

Silvia (1) _____*can*_____ type. She (2) _____ answer the phone,

and she (3) _____ talk with customers. Silvia (4) _____ file,

and she (5) _____ fax.

 Exercise 4: In your notebook complete the sentences about you.
Write what you *can* and *can't* do.
For example, write, "I can't type. I can file."

  Your Turn

Roy works with Silvia. Study the chart. Talk with a partner. Tell what Roy
can and can't do. For example, say, "Roy can answer the phone."

ROY CAN	ROY CAN'T
answer the phone	type
fax	write to customers
help customers	file

SPOTLIGHT ON *CAN* IN YES/NO QUESTIONS AND SHORT ANSWERS

Statements and Yes/No Questions	Short Answers
He can answer telephones.	
Can he answer telephones?	Yes, **he can**. No, **he can't**.
They can answer telephones.	
Can they answer telephones?	Yes, **they can**. No, **they can't**.

Can is the same for all persons (*I, you, he, she, it, we, they*).
Put *can* first to make questions.

Exercise 5: Study the story about Silvia again.
Complete each question and write a short answer.

1. __Can__ Silvia type? Yes, __she can.__

2. _____ she answer the phone? Yes, _____.

3. _____ she write to customers? No, _____.

4. _____ Silvia fax? No, _____.

Person to Person

Listen to the conversation. Then practice it with a partner.

MANAGER: I have your job application. Can you type and file?

SURUPA: Yes, I can. And I can fax and answer phones.

Your Turn

Study the conversation. With a partner write a new conversation about an office clerk who wants a job.
Share your conversation with other students.

With your teacher and other students, talk about the words below.

right   skills   private

READING FOR REAL

Carl wants to ask for a raise. He's reading about how to ask for a raise.

How to Ask for a Raise

✔ Talk to your supervisor. He or she knows your skills.

✔ Ask in the right place. Use an office or a private place.

✔ Ask at the right time. Don't ask at a busy moment.

✔ Talk about your job skills. Tell about what you can do.

Exercise 6: Think about the reading. Circle *yes*, *no*, or *not sure*. With a partner compare your answers.

1. Carl's reading about how to ask for a road map.

   yes   (no)   not sure

2. You can ask a clerk for a raise.

   yes   no   not sure

3. A good time is when it's quiet.

   yes   no   not sure

4. The right place is a restaurant.

   yes   no   not sure

5. Tell about what you can do.

   yes   no   not sure

Talk About It

Why does Carl need a raise?
Is asking for a raise easy or hard? Why?

With your teacher and other students, talk about the words below.

minimum wage   pay   government   sometimes   change

CULTURE CORNER

Many workers in the United States get only the minimum wage. This is a minimum amount of money for an hour of work. The U.S. government tells businesses how much to pay. The businesses pay the workers. Sometimes the government changes the minimum wage. Then the workers get a raise.

YEAR	MINIMUM WAGE PER HOUR
1938	$.25
1950	$.75
1963	$1.25
1975	$2.10
1980	$3.10
1997	$5.15

Exercise 7: Write the minimum-wage raises in the blanks. With another student compare your answers.

YEARS	MINIMUM WAGE RAISES
1938–1950	$ .50
1950–1963	
1963–1975	
1975–1980	
1980–1997	

In Your Experience

In a group talk about the minimum-wage. Ask the questions below.
Then share your answers with the class. How much is the minimum wage now?
Is the minimum wage good pay? Why or why not?
How much do you think workers need for the minimum wage?

S C E N E 2

Talk about the pictures. Ask and answer the questions.

Carl needs more skills to get a raise. He talks to Mr. Khong.

Mr. Khong, can we talk now?

Sure, Carl.

I can use a calculator, answer phones, file, and fax. But where can I learn computer skills?

Well, North Community College has classes on weekends.

Questions

What does Carl ask?

What can Carl do?

What are your skills?

What can you do?

V O C A B U L A R Y   P R O M P T S

With your teacher and other students, talk about the words below.

learn   weekend   weekdays   community college   birthday

Office Work

use a computer

use a calculator

use a copy machine

write memos

order supplies

Your words

_____

SPOTLIGHT ON PREPOSITIONS OF TIME

on	in	at

We can talk **on** Monday   **in** January   **at** 7:00

              on weekends   **in** 1999

              on weekdays

              on March 13

Use *on*, *in*, or *at* to answer the question *When?*

Exercise 8: Complete the story about Berta with *on*, *in*, or *at*. With another student compare your answers.

(1) ___On___ weekdays Berta works in an office.

She goes to work (2) _____ 8:00.

She goes home (3) _____ 4:30.

She orders supplies (4) _____ January and July.

She mails cards (5) _____ December.

She buys a new business license (6) _____ April.

Berta goes on vacation (7) _____ June.

Exercise 9: In your notebook write 7 new sentences.
Tell what you do on weekdays.
Tell what you do in different months.

Person to Person

Listen to the conversation. Then practice it with a partner.

JODY: My birthday is in July. It's on July 17.

TRAN: My birthday isn't in July. It's in December.
It's on December 15.

Your Turn

Work with a partner. Study the conversation.
Write a conversation about your birthdays.
Share your conversation with the class.

GET GRAPHIC

Carl is a clerk with good office skills. But now he wants a new job, and he needs *more* skills. He wants to go to weekend classes. He's making a chart. He's checking his skills and the things he wants to learn. Read his chart.

skills	I can	I want to learn to
type		✔
answer phones	✔	
use a calculator		✔
write memos		✔
file	✔	
use a copy machine	✔	
use computer programs		✔
order supplies	✔	
fax	✔	

Your Turn

With a partner talk about what Carl can and can't do.

Exercise 10: Write the words from Column B in the sentences in Column A.

COLUMN A

1. Carl can use a _____ calculator _____

2. Carl can't use a _____

   or write _____

3. Carl wants to use a _____

   and order _____

4. Carl wants to learn 5 new _____

COLUMN B

computer, supplies

skills

copy machine, memos

calculator

In Your Experience

Study Carl's chart. Then make your own chart.
List your job skills. Then list skills you want to learn.
Share your chart with other students.
Talk about where you can learn more skills in your community.

ISSUES AND ANSWERS

Read the letters. Then talk with other students about the answer.
Tell what you think. Is the answer good or bad? Why?

 **Ask ABDUL and ANITA**

DEAR ABDUL,

I have a family and many bills. I have a good job, but I need a raise. When I ask my supervisor for a raise, she tells me she is not sure. What can I do?

CAN'T PAY THE BILLS

DEAR CAN'T PAY,

Are you a good worker? What are your skills? Write a memo to your supervisor. Write about your skills and your plans to learn more. In your memo ask for a raise. Tell how much you want per hour. Give her time to think about it. Ask for a memo with her answer.

ABDUL

Think About Learning

Check (✔) to show your learning in this unit.
Write one more thing at the bottom.

SKILLS / STRUCTURES	Page	easy ☺	so-so ☹	difficult ☹
Read "How to Ask for a Raise"	65			
Talk about the minimum wage	66			
Read a skills chart	69			
Talk about the skills you want	69			
Tell what you think	69			
Make an idea map	70			
Use *can* in statements	63			
Use *can* in yes/no questions and short answers	64			
Use prepositions of time	68			

WATCHING TV

S C E N E 1

Talk about the pictures. Ask and answer the questions.

Steve and Tim are on break at work. They're talking about TV.

The football game was on TV yesterday, right?

Right, the big game!

What was the score? Was it 24 to 21?

I don't know. We weren't home. My wife doesn't like football.

Questions

When was the game on TV?
Does Tim's wife like football?

Do you like to watch football on TV?

V O C A B U L A R Y   P R O M P T S

With your teacher and other students, talk about the words below.

on break   score   big   game   yesterday

Team Sports on TV

baseball

basketball

football

hockey

soccer

Your words

_____

 ## SOUND BITES

Exercise 1: Listen. Find the picture. Circle *a* or *b*.

1.
a.   (b.)

2.
a.   b.

3.
a.   b.

4.
a.   b.

  Your Turn

Listen again and repeat.

SPOTLIGHT ON PAST OF *BE* IN AFFIRMATIVE STATEMENTS

I **was** home yesterday.   You **were** home yesterday.

He   We

She   They

It

In the past, *be* has two forms—*was* and *were*.

Exercise 2: Complete the story about Ava and Ben with the past of *be*.

Yesterday, Ava and Ben (1) __were__ at work. Ben (2) _____ at his office.

He (3) _____ busy. Ava _____ (4) at the hotel. Her job (5) _____

hard. They (6) _____ happy to go home at 5:00 and watch sports on TV!

Exercise 3: In your notebook rewrite the story below.
Use the past instead of the present.

It is Saturday. Amir, Fatima, and their children are at home.
Amir is in the garage. He is busy with the car. Fatima is in the house.
She is busy in her home office. The children are in front of the TV.
They are happy to watch a soccer game!

Person to Person

Listen to the conversation. Then practice it with a partner.

NINA: I was on vacation yesterday.

JOHN: You were at the big baseball game in Atlanta, right?

NINA: Yes. It was 82° and sunny! And it was a good game!

Your Turn

Study the conversation. With a partner write a new conversation.
Use a different city, temperature, weather, and sport.
Share your new conversation with other students.

In Your Experience

Talk in a group of students. Talk about yesterday.
Where were you? What was the temperature?
What was the weather like?
Were you busy? Was it a good day?

SPOTLIGHT ON PAST OF *BE* IN NEGATIVE STATEMENTS

I	**was not**	home yesterday.	You	**were not**	home yesterday.
He	(wasn't)		We	(weren't)	
She			They		
(It)					

Exercise 4: Read the story in your notebook about Ava and Ben (from Exercise 2 on page 73). Then write it below. Change the verbs to the negative. Use *wasn't* or *weren't*.

_____

_____

_____

_____

_____

Exercise 5: In your notebook change the story below about Alex, a waiter in a restaurant. Write the story in the negative. Use *wasn't* or *weren't*.

It was a good day for Alex yesterday. It was sunny. He was happy about the weather. At work the manager was happy because the waiters were ready to take food orders at 12:00 noon. And the customers were happy because the service was fast and the food was good!

Person to Person

Listen to the conversation. Then practice it with a partner.

JOE: Yesterday's game wasn't good! My brothers and I sure weren't happy about the score!

KIM: Oh? My friends and I weren't home to watch it. But it wasn't our favorite football team.

JOE: Well, it sure wasn't our favorite team yesterday!

Your Turn

Study the conversation. Talk with a partner. Ask and answer these questions. Were you home on the weekend? Was your favorite team on TV?

Talk about the words with your teacher and other students.

show   channel   news   program guide   hour

READING FOR REAL

A program guide gives the names, TV channels, and times of programs.
Read the program guide for Saturday night.

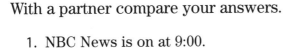

PROGRAM GUIDE – SATURDAY NIGHT						
CHANNEL	**7:00**	**7:30**	**8:00**	**8:30**	**9:00**	**9:30**
2	NBC News		The Sampsons		Tom Talk Show	
4	Saturday Movie: A Father for Joe		CBS Sports: Football			
5	Movie Favorite: Kerby, the Car		ABC Sports: Baseball			
6	English on TV		Healthy Eating			

Exercise 6: Think about the program guide. Circle *yes*, *no*, or *not sure*.
With a partner compare your answers.

1. NBC News is on at 9:00.

   yes   (no)   not sure

2. The Channel 4 movie is *Healthy Eating*.

   yes   no   not sure

3. *English on TV* is a two-hour show.

   yes   no   not sure

4. Football is on ABC at 9:00.

   yes   no   not sure

5. Channels 4 and 5 have sports at 9:00.

   yes   no   not sure

Talk About It

Do you use a program guide at home? How do you use it?

With your teacher and other students, talk about the words below.

free   all   every year   type

CULTURE CORNER

In the United States many TV channels are free. People can get free
TV channels all day, every day of the year. But cable TV is not free.
People pay for cable TV. People love their favorite channels.
And some people are happy to pay for them.

TOP THREE U.S. CABLE TV CHANNELS	TYPE OF PROGRAM	NUMBER OF CUSTOMERS
1. ESPN	sports	67,100,000
2. CNN	news	66,600,000
3. TBS	movies	66,500,000

Exercise 7: What are your favorite types of programs—sports, news,
or movies? Look at the chart above and answer.

MY TOP THREE TYPES OF PROGRAMS	CABLE TV CHANNEL
1.	1.
2.	2.
3.	3.

In Your Experience

With your class look at the chart. Write questions like the first question.
Then find the answers to the questions in the chart. Then, with a partner
talk about what you like.

	QUESTION	ANSWER
1. have cable TV	How many students have cable TV?	
2. like team sports on TV		
3. like movies on TV		
4. like news on TV		
5. like other TV programs		

S C E N E **2**

Talk about the pictures. Ask and answer the questions.

Steve, Tim, and José are on break at work. They're talking about TV.

Were you at the game yesterday, José?

No, I wasn't. I was home in front of the TV.

OK! So was the score 24-21?

I didn't watch the game. Two great movies were on cable.

Questions

Where was José yesterday?
Does José know the score?
Why or why not?

Do you watch movies on cable TV?

V O C A B U L A R Y   P R O M P T S

With your teacher and other students, talk about the words below.

after   great   television

Television Programs

soap opera / drama

talk show

cartoon

comedy

educational program

Your words

_____

Was	he home yesterday?	Yes, he	**was.**	No, he	**wasn't.**
	she	she		she	
Were	we home yesterday?	Yes, we	**were.**	No, we	**weren't.**
	you	you		you	
	they	they		they	

Exercise 8: Read the story about José. Then complete the yes/no questions and answers about the story.

José was home on Friday night. His wife and children were home too.
They were in front of the TV for three hours.
Some great programs were on. A comedy was on at 7:00.
A drama was on at 8:00. The news was on after the drama.

1. __Was__ José at home on Friday night? Yes, he __was__.

2. _____ José's wife and children at home too? Yes, they _____.

3. _____ the comedy on at 9:00? No, it _____.

4. _____ the news on after the drama? Yes, it _____.

Exercise 9: In your notebook write 2 more yes/no questions about José and his family. Then write the answers.

Your Turn

Read the chart with a partner. Complete the questions.
Ask and answer the questions. Then fill out the chart.

QUESTIONS		PARTNER 1		PARTNER 2	
		yes	no	yes	no
1. *Were you*	home on Friday night?				
2.	the TV on?				
3.	a comedy on TV?				
4.	a drama on TV?				
5.	sports on TV?				

With your teacher and other students, talk about the words below.

before   information   evening

GET GRAPHIC

Many of the students at the Brown School for Adult Learning watch TV with their families on weekend and weekday evenings. Read the chart for information.

AVERAGE TIME PER WEEK WATCHING TELEVISION		
	Weekday evenings before 10 P.M.	Weekend evenings before 10 P.M.
Women	1 1/2 hours	2 1/2 hours
Men	2 hours	3 hours
Children	2 hours	3 1/2 hours

Exercise 10: Write the numbers from Column B in the sentences in Column A.

COLUMN A   COLUMN B

1. The women watch for ___1 1/2 hours___ on weekdays.   5 hours

2. The men watch for _____ on weekdays.   2 hours

3. The men watch for _____ every week   1 1/2 hours
   (weekends and weekdays).
                                                           5 1/2 hours

4. The children watch _____ every week.

In Your Experience

In your notebook write the number of hours you watch TV every week. Share your information with the class.
Then ask and answer the following questions.
Is too much TV bad for people? Why or why not?
What programs do you watch on weekdays and weekends?
What programs do you watch in English?

WRAP-UP

With a group make an idea map. Talk about television programs you watched last week. Were they good or just so-so? Why?

Good Programs   So-so Programs

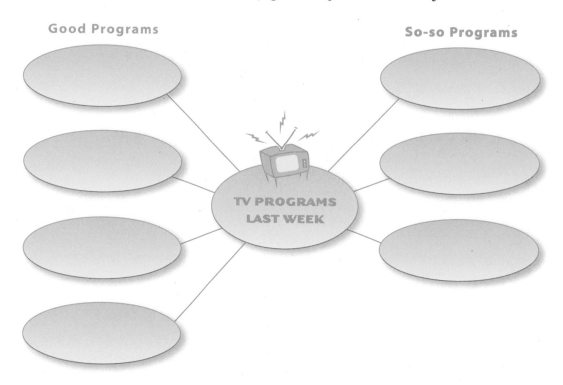

TV PROGRAMS
LAST WEEK

Think About Learning

Check (✔) to show your learning in this unit. Write one more thing at the bottom.

SKILLS / STRUCTURES	Page	easy ☺	so-so 😐	difficult ☹
Read a schedule	75			
Read a TV program guide	75			
Make a Top Three List of my favorite cable channels	76			
Read a chart of averages	79			
Write the number of hours a week I watch TV	79			
Make an idea map	80			
Use past of *be* in affirmative statements	73			
Use past of *be* in negative statements	74			
Use past of *be* in yes/no questions and short answers	78			

Talk about the pictures. Ask and answer the questions.

After work Donna and Alicia are talking about school.

Questions

Who passed the GED Test?
What did Alicia want to do?

What do you want to study?

VOCABULARY PROMPTS

With your teacher and other students, talk about the words below.

GED Test   pass   finish   smart   study

School Subjects

math

history

English

science

art

Your words

_____

 # SOUND BITES

Exercise 1: Listen. Find the picture. Circle *a* or *b*.

1.

a.   b.

2.

a.   b.

3.

a.   b.

4.

a.   b.

   Your Turn

Listen again and repeat.

SPOTLIGHT ON SIMPLE PAST IN AFFIRMATIVE STATEMENTS

I / You / He / She / We / You / They   **passed** the test.   We   **passed** the test.

Many verbs are regular. Regular verbs have *-ed* in the past.
The following verbs are irregular:

Present	Past	Present	Past
do	did	have	had
come	came	go	went
make	made	write	wrote
get	got	take	took
feel	felt		

Exercise 2: Complete John's story with simple past.
Change the *italic* words to the correct forms.

John (1) *want* ____wanted____ to finish high school. He (2) *talk* _____

with a teacher at Green Adult School. He (3) *ask* _____ about GED

classes. The teacher (4) *help* _____ John study English, history, math,

and science. John (5) *work* _____ hard for two years. He (6) *pass*

_____ the GED Test. John (7) *finish* _____ high school!

Exercise 3: Write Susana's story in your notebook. Put the verbs
in the past tense. Change the *italic* words to the correct forms.

Susana (1) *want* to study history. She (2) *ask* a counselor about classes
at a community college. The counselor (3) *help* her. He (4) *talk* with her.
He (5) *answer* all her questions. Then she (6) *start* a history class.
Susana (7) *like* the class.

Person to Person

Listen to the conversation. Then practice it with a partner.

JAN: Yesterday was a hard day. I wrote a story and went to class.

PAT: I was sick, so I went home. But I studied in the evening.

Your Turn

Study the conversation. With a partner, write a new conversation
about two students in your English class. Use regular and irregular
past tense. Share your conversation with other students.

SPOTLIGHT ON SIMPLE PAST IN NEGATIVE STATEMENTS

I/You/He/She/We/They/ **did not** finish school.
(didn't)

To make past-tense verbs negative, use *did not* + verb.

Exercise 4: Complete the story. Use simple past negative statements. Put the *italic* words into the correct forms.

Rick (1) *finish* _____didn't finish_____ high school.

He (2) *like* _____ the subjects, so he (3) *want*

_____ to study. Rick went to class, but he (4) *learn*

_____ much. He (5) *study* _____

and he (6) *pass* _____ the tests!

Exercise 5: Write this story in your notebook. Use simple past negatives. Use the correct form of each *italic* word. For example, write, "Barbara didn't go to class yesterday."

Barbara (1) *go* to class yesterday because she (2) *have* time. She (3) *get* home from work before 6:30. Then she cooked dinner for her children. They (4) *eat* before 7:00. The class was at 7:00, so Barbara (5) *go* to it.

Person to Person

Listen to the conversation. Then practice it with a partner.

KEN: I didn't see you in art class yesterday. Were you sick?

AMY No. I was home with my children. I didn't have a babysitter. What did you do in class?

KEN: We learned about color, but we didn't make anything.

Your Turn

Study the conversation. With a partner write a new conversation about two students in a class. Use simple past negatives.
Share your conversation with other students.

In Your Experience

Think about a time when you didn't go to class. Why didn't you go? Write your answer with simple past negatives. Share your answer with a group.

With your teacher and other students, talk about the words below.

chapter   page   pilot   poet   life

READING FOR REAL

A table of contents is in the front of a book. The table of contents
lists the chapters and page numbers. Read the table of contents
for *Great American Women*.

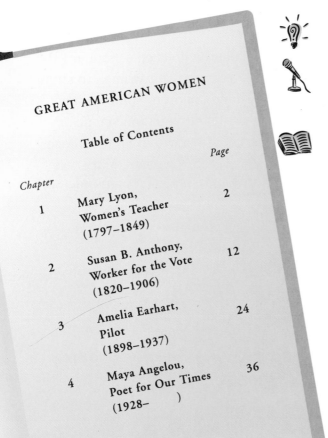

GREAT AMERICAN WOMEN

Table of Contents

Exercise 6: Think about the table
of contents. Circle *yes*, *no*, or *not sure*.
With a partner compare your answers.

1. Chapter 2 is about Maya Angelou.

   yes   (no)   not sure

2. Chapter 3 is about a woman pilot.

   yes   no   not sure

3. Susan B. Anthony lived after 1800.

   yes   no   not sure

4. Mary Lyon helped women before 1700.

   yes   no   not sure

5. Chapter 4 is about a woman poet.

   yes   no   not sure

Talk About It

What chapters do you want to read? Why?
Did you study history in school? What did you study?

VOCABULARY PROMPTS

With your teacher and other students, talk about the words below.

born   stay   died   started   soon

CULTURE CORNER

Read the story. Then, in your notebook answer the
questions with sentences from the story.

MARY LYON, WOMEN'S TEACHER

Mary Lyon was born in 1797. She was smart. She finished school in 1814.
Mary was a teacher. In 1800 many people did not want women to study.
People wanted women to stay home with the children. Some women
learned to read and write. But they did not learn math and science.
They did not go to college. Mary Lyon wanted women to go to college.
In 1837 Mary started Mount Holyoke, a college for women. Mary was
the principal. At Mount Holyoke women studied English, math, history,
and science.

Mary Lyon died in 1849. Soon more colleges for women opened
in America. Now men and women go to the same schools.
They study the same subjects. Mary Lyon helped to change schools
in the United States.

1. Why didn't people want women to study in 1800?
   People wanted women to stay home with the children.

2. What subjects didn't women learn in 1800?

3. What did Mary Lyon start in 1837?

4. What subjects did women study at Mount Holyoke?

In Your Experience

Talk with a partner. Answer the questions below.
Tell what you think. Share your answers with a group.
What subjects do men and women need to study now? Why?
Now some people don't finish school. Why not?
Where can they finish school?

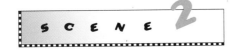

Talk about the pictures. Ask and answer the questions.

Donna is studying at home. Her husband is asking her questions.

Did you buy food today?

No, I didn't. I studied. I have a test tomorrow.

Why didn't you shop first and then study?

I didn't have time.

Questions

Did Donna shop for food today?
What did Donna do today?

Who shops for food at your house?

V O C A B U L A R Y   P R O M P T S

With your teacher and other students, talk about the words below.

first   this week   today   tomorrow   because

Today's Women

politics

education

health

law

business

Your words

SPOTLIGHT ON SIMPLE PAST YES/NO QUESTIONS, SHORT ANSWERS, AND INFORMATION QUESTIONS

Yes/No Questions

Did	you	**buy** groceries?
	he	
	she	
	we	
	they	

Short Answers

Yes,	I	**did.**	No,	I	**didn't.**
	he			he	
	she			she	
	we			we	
	they			they	

Information Questions

When	did	I	buy groceries?
Where		you	
How		he	
Why		she	
		we	
		they	

Who	did	I	ask?
What		you	
		he	
		she	
		we	
		they	

Exercise 7: Donna's husband is asking a lot of questions. In your notebook write yes/no questions for Donna's answers.

1. <u>Did you buy food today?</u>
   No, I didn't. I didn't buy food today.
2. Yes, I did. I studied at home today.
3. No, I didn't. I didn't pay the bills.
4. Yes, I did. I cooked dinner.

Exercise 8: Read the story below. In your notebook write an information question for each answer about David's life yesterday.

David went to English class yesterday. He learned irregular verbs in class. After class he studied verbs at home because he wanted more practice. At 5:30 David's wife came home from work. David and his wife cooked dinner. After dinner his wife helped him study irregular verbs.

1. <u>Where did David go yesterday?</u>
   He went **to English class.**
2. He learned **irregular verbs.**
3. He studied verbs at home **because he wanted more practice.**
4. **David's wife** came home.
5. She came home **at 5:30.**
6. They **cooked dinner.**
7. **His wife** helped him study irregular verbs.

With your teacher and other students, talk about the words below.

events   right   vote   allow   laws

GET GRAPHIC

A time line shows dates and events. Read the time line about
Susan B. Anthony, a worker for the vote.

Before 1920 many Americans did not want women to think about
politics. Men had the right to vote, but women did not.
Susan B. Anthony wanted American women to have the right
to vote. She worked with other women to change the laws.
The new laws gave women the right to vote.

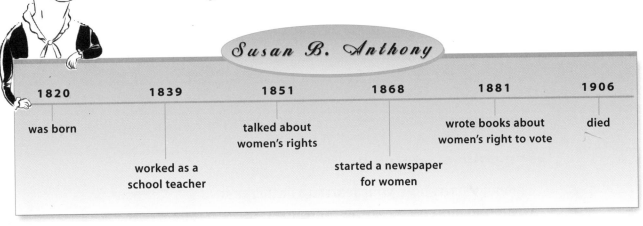

Susan B. Anthony

1820	1839	1851	1868	1881	1906
was born		talked about women's rights		wrote books about women's right to vote	died
	worked as a school teacher		started a newspaper for women		

Exercise 9: Write information from Column B in the sentences in Column A.

COLUMN A   COLUMN B

1. Susan B. Anthony was born in _____1820_____.   1851

2. In 1868, she wrote a newspaper for _____.   died

3. Susan B. Anthony _____ in 1906.   1820

4. She started to work for women's rights in _____.   women

In Your Experience

On a large piece of paper, make a time line of your life.
Write the dates and important events of your life.
Share your time line with your class.

ISSUES AND ANSWERS

Read the letters. Then talk with other students about
the answer. Is the answer good or bad? What other things
can "Sorry Now" do?

 *Ask ABDUL and ANITA*

DEAR ANITA,

I wasn't a good student in school.
I didn't go to all my classes, and I
didn't study. I didn't finish my education.
Now I want to learn more about
politics and law. I want to know about
my rights, but I don't have time to go
to school. How can I learn more now?

SORRY NOW

DEAR SORRY,

You can do many things to learn
more now! Watch TV. Read a program
guide for shows about history, politics,
and law. Read newspapers and books.
Community groups can help too. Call
the League of Women Voters. Ask the
League about events in your city.

ANITA

Think About Learning

Check (✔) to show your learning in this unit.
Write one more thing at the bottom.

SKILLS / STRUCTURES	Page	easy ☺	so-so 😐	difficult ☹
Read a table of contents	85			
Read about Mary Lyon	86			
Read a time line	89			
Make a time line	89			
Tell what you think	90			
Use simple past affirmative statements	83			
Use simple past negative statements	84			
Use simple past questions and short answers	88			

CARDS AND MACHINES

SCENE 1

Talk about the pictures. Ask and answer the questions.

Marisol is going to visit her sister in Mexico.
Her father is giving her a phone card for long-distance calls.

> Marisol, this is a long-distance phone card to use in Cancún.

> Thanks, Dad! I'm going to call my friends here and in Mexico City.

> And when are you going to call me?

> Oh, I'm not going to forget you, Dad.

Questions

What does Marisol's father give her?
Who is Marisol going to call?

Do you have a phone card?
What other cards do you have?

VOCABULARY PROMPTS

With your teacher and other students, talk about the words below.

visit   forget   long distance   leave   clean

Using the Telephone

phone card

touch-tone phone

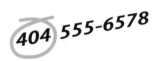

404 *555-6578*

area code

phone number

rotary phone

Your words

_____

SOUND BITES

Exercise 1: Listen. Find the picture. Circle *a* or *b*.

1.

a.   b.

2.

a.   b.

3.

a.   b.

4.

a.   b.

Your Turn

Listen again and repeat.

SPOTLIGHT ON FUTURE WITH *GOING TO* IN STATEMENTS

Affirmative

I	**am going to**	call Liz.
He/She/(It)	**is going to**	
You/We/They	**are going to**	

Negative

I	**am not going to** get a card.
He/She/(It)	**is not going to**
You/We/They	**are not going to**

Affirmative with Contractions

I'm / You're / He's / She's / (It's) / We're / They're going to finish the job.

Negative with Contractions

I'm	**not going to**	work tomorrow.
We're/You're/They're	OR	We **aren't**/You **aren't**/They **aren't going to** talk to him.
He's/She's/(It's)	OR	He/She **isn't going to**

Use *going to* + a verb to talk about things that will happen in the future.

 Exercise 2: Read the story.

Marisol is going to go to Mexico. She is going to leave tomorrow.
She is going to stay with her sister. They are going to see family and friends.
Marisol isn't going to study in a school in Mexico, and she isn't going to have a job.
She is going to visit for just one month.

 Exercise 3: Work with a partner. In your notebook write the sentences about Marisol and her sister. Use *is going to, isn't going to, are going to,* or *aren't going to.*

Example: Marisol is going to go to Mexico.

  Person to Person

Listen to the conversation. Then practice it with a partner.

SILVIA: On Saturday I'm not going to shop for anything new.
I'm going to clean the garage.

NICK: OK! I'm not going to watch the football game on TV.
I'm going to help you!

  Your Turn

With a partner write a new conversation about what you're going to do on Saturday. Share it with other students.

SPOTLIGHT ON FUTURE WITH *GOING TO* IN YES/NO QUESTIONS, SHORT ANSWERS, AND INFORMATION QUESTIONS

Yes/No Questions

Am	I	**going to** call your friends?
Is	he	
	she	
Are	you	
	we	
	they	

Short Answers

Yes,	I	**am.**	No,	**I'm**	**not.**
	he	**is.**		**he's**	**not.**
	she			**she**	**isn't.**
	you	**are.**		**you**	**aren't.**
	we			**we**	
	they			**they**	

Information Questions

Who	am I going to call?	**Who**	is he	going to call?	**Who**	are	you going to call?
When		**When**	she		**When**		we
Where		**Where**			**Where**		they
Why		**Why**			**Why**		
How		**How**			**How**		

Exercise 4: Reread the story about Marisol and her sister on page 93. Write yes/no questions. Check your questions with a partner. Talk about questions that are different.

1. _____*Is*_____ Marisol _____*going to go*_____ to Mexico?
   Yes, she is. She is going to go to Mexico.

2. _____ she _____ with her sister?
   Yes, she is. She is going to stay with her sister.

3. _____ they _____ their friends?
   Yes, they are. Marisol and her sister are going to visit their friends.

4. _____ she _____ a job?
   No, she isn't. She isn't going to have a job.

Exercise 5: With your partner look at the answers below and complete the questions.

1. _____*When is*_____ she _____*going to go*_____?
   She is going to go tomorrow.

2. _____ she _____?
   She is going to stay with her sister.

3. _____ they _____?
   They are going to see family and friends.

With your teacher and other students, talk about the words below.

PIN number   press   country code   steps   international

READING FOR REAL

This is Marisol's phone card. Read the steps on the card.

Phone card

Easy Steps:

1. Press 1 800 666-7777

2. Press your PIN number: 234 5678 890

3. Press 1 + area code + number
   (International calls press 2 + country code + number

Exercise 6: Think about the phone card. Circle *yes, no,* or *not sure.*
With a partner compare your answers.

1. There are three steps.

   (yes)   no   not sure

2. Press 1 800 667-7777 first.

   yes   no   not sure

3. Press your PIN Number after
   1 + area code + number.

   yes   no   not sure

4. For international calls press
   2 + country code + number.

   yes   no   not sure

5. The PIN number is your phone number.

   yes   no   not sure

Talk About It

Is a phone card easy to use? Why or why not?
How do you pay for your long-distance calls?

VOCABULARY PROMPTS

With your teacher and other students, talk about the words below.

computer chip   bank   airport

CULTURE CORNER

Read the article.

SMART CARDS

In the future, smart cards are going to make life easy for Americans. Smart cards have a computer chip. The computer chip has information about the customer (name, social security number, address, phone number, health information, bank information). You are going to use your smart card at stores, airports, hotels, hospitals, banks, and restaurants. You are going to use your smart card to give information and pay bills. Smart cards are going to help you get fast service.

Your Turn

Check (✔) the chart. With a partner compare your answers.
Talk about the answers that are different.

	Smart cards are going to help.	Smart cards aren't going to help.	Not sure
1. People want fast service.			
2. Workers need more jobs.			
3. Customers have to pay bills.			
4. Hospitals need health information.			
5. Americans like fast cars.			

In Your Experience

In a small group write questions to ask other students. Ask questions and complete the chart. Share your chart with your class and talk about the answers.

NUMBER OF ANSWERS	MEN		WOMEN	
	Yes	No	Yes	No
1. He/she has a phone card now.				
2. He/she is going to get a phone card soon.				
3. He/she is going to get a smart card in the future.				

Talk about the pictures. Ask and answer the questions.

Marisol's father is giving her another card.

Here's another card. It's an ATM card for emergency cash.

Dad, this is great, but I don't know how to use it!

Questions

What card is Marisol's father giving her?
Does Marisol know how to use the card?

How do you use cards with machines?

VOCABULARY PROMPTS

With your teacher and other students, talk about the words below.

here's   another   emergency   cash

Cards and Machines

credit card

ATM card

key card

grocery discount card

gas card

Your words

_____

SPOTLIGHT ON COMPOUND SENTENCES

Two Sentences

Marisol has a phone card.
She's getting an ATM card.

She can get cash from a bank.
She can use an ATM.

Marisol likes the ATM card.
She doesn't know how to use it.

One Compound Sentence

Marisol has a phone card, **and** she's getting an ATM card.

She can get cash from a bank, **or** she can use an ATM.

Marisol likes the ATM card, **but** she doesn't know how to use it.

You can use the words *and*, *or*, and *but* to make two sentences into one sentence.

Exercise 7: Write the story about Daniel in your notebook.
Use *and*, *but*, and *or* to make compound sentences. Then, with a partner compare your answers. Help your partner correct any errors.

1. *(and)* Daniel wants to go to Canada.   He plans to visit his family.

   Daniel wants to go to Canada, and he plans to visit his family.

2. *(or)* He can stay with his brother.   He can stay with his sister.

   _____

3. *(but)* He wants to drive his car.   The car needs new tires.

   _____

4. *(and)* He can go to Canada.   He can buy new tires.

   _____

Person to Person

Listen to the conversation. Then practice it with a partner.

JOEL: I want to study English, but I have to work!

LISA: You can try evening classes at adult school, or you can go to a community college on Saturdays. You can work, and you can learn English!

Your Turn

Study the conversation.
With a partner write a new conversation with compound sentences.
Share your conversation with other students.

With your teacher and other students, talk about the words below.

pay phone   collect call   savings   phone company   coin

GET GRAPHIC

Read about the *PhoneCard Plus* phone card. The bar graph shows savings with the phone card for a 3-minute call.

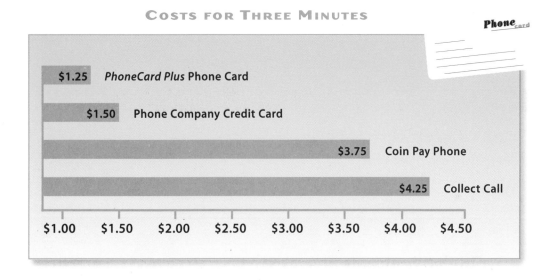

COSTS FOR THREE MINUTES

$1.25	*PhoneCard Plus* Phone Card
$1.50	Phone Company Credit Card
$3.75	Coin Pay Phone
$4.25	Collect Call

$1.00 $1.50 $2.00 $2.50 $3.00 $3.50 $4.00 $4.50

Exercise 8: Write the information from Column B in the sentences in Column A.

COLUMN A	COLUMN B
1. A 3-minute phone-card call costs ___$1.25___.	$3.75
2. A 3-minute coin pay-phone call costs _____.	$1.25
3. A 3-minute phone company credit-card call costs _____.	$1.50
4. A 3-minute collect call costs _____.	$4.25

In Your Experience

Talk in a group of 3. Tell your classmates about your phone calls. Answer their questions. Do you call long distance? When? Why? How do you pay for the calls? How long do you talk?

WRAP-UP

With a group make a T–chart. Talk about computers of the future.
What are they going to do? When?

COMPUTERS OF THE FUTURE

IN 5 YEARS	IN 10 YEARS
Computers, not clerks, are going to help customers in some stores.	

Think About Learning

Check (✔) to show your learning in this unit.
Write one more thing at the bottom.

SKILLS / STRUCTURES	Page	easy 🙂	so-so 😐	difficult ☹
Read steps for using a phone card	95			
Read about smart cards	96			
Read a bar graph	99			
Ask about phone cards and make a chart	96			
Make an idea map about computers	100			
Use future with *going to* in statements	93			
Use future with *going to* in questions	94			
Use compound sentences	98			